PLANET DRAG

PLANET DRAG

UNCOVER THE GLOBAL HERSTORY

Curated by COURTNEY CONQUERS

Foreword by BROOKE LYNN HYTES

WHITE LION PUBLISHING

CONTENTS

FOREWORD

I began dancing at the age of 13 and I've been an artist ever since. Through my time in *Les Ballets Trocadero de Monte Carlo*, I've been getting into drag since long before I actually became a drag queen. Yet, no matter how many years I'm involved in the art of drag, it never fails to astonish me. Even compared to my own past industries, the strength, skill, and wit of the drag performers I know stands unparalleled. The fortitude it takes to stay funny, fierce and thriving in the face of international scrutiny – especially in an arena that existed outside the mainstream's gaze for so long – takes courage. Living and working at the centre of drag's most unprecedented surge has been a privilege I never anticipated.

As thrilled as I am to see drag take firmer footing in pop culture, I know first-hand that such success comes at a price. Transphobic political agendas disguised as anti-drag bills have stoked right-wing fires against queer artists. Meanwhile, bigger platforms for drag queens – but mostly for very certain kinds – have highlighted inequities within the drag industry itself. As such, values like community and visibility have become more important than ever before. Mutual support between artists and allyship from drag's supporters are some of our strongest weapons against those who would see our art (and, quite frankly, our kind) eradicated if they could. Drag has *always* been political, but its authentic global necessity remains as pivotal today as ever.

The power of drag serves to benefit people the world over, so why not take a look at its international impact? *Planet Drag* celebrates the drag of 15 countries; some places you've probably seen on your favourite TV shows and others that deserve the same recognition and opportunity as their counterparts. The way Courtney and her contributors have showcased the history of these drag scenes brings to life not just the courage deployed by drag's founding mothers (and fathers, aunties and uncles), but also how their trailblazing continues impacting our work in drag today. I am always conscious, particularly on the judging panel, of the ways in which drag history remains intrinsic to what artists like me showcase today.

If drag is an act of resistance (and it is!) then *Planet Drag* is a battle cry from within its numbers. Courtney and her authors – all of whom study, support or actually do drag – exemplify drag's tenacity and highlight its diversity right from the roots in an effort to teach us about the road drag has travelled on its journey to our screens and beyond.

Enjoy these true tales of wonder and woe and remember: Drag is *for* everyone, it's done *by* everyone, and it isn't going anywhere!

Brooke Lynn Hytes

DISRUPTING THE NORM AROUND THE WORLD

COURTNEY CONQUERS

ALL DRAGGED UP

I recall very clearly the first time I saw drag queens. As a child, I was often at home nursing chronic migraines while my mom performed the (shockingly numerous) duties of being a Royal Canadian Air Force spouse. As such, I was exposed to more daytime television than I'm sure either of us thought twice about. That's how I discovered RuPaul Charles and Varla Jean Merman – now legends, but in the mid-1990s just two young drag queens trying to make an impact in New York City. I encountered them on one of those daytime chat shows, part informational, part pop-cultural and part 'special interest', with segments that (occasionally problematically) highlighted the oddities of humanity – those who live differently from the average viewer.

RuPaul and Varla were the most glamorous women I'd ever seen, and I was enthralled. They discussed fashion with the host, and their inclusion in the segment hinged on scathingly humorous commentary on celebrity outfits and hot new trends; the kinds of joke that other people might not get away with but drag queens have always had license to make, to raucous laughter. I don't remember when it dawned on me that these guests were not the 'conventional', albeit loudly made-up, women I thought they were, but I do recall my innocently simple reaction: 'Huh. Cool!' I ogled their long nails, thick lipstick and backcombed hair until my mom absentmindedly changed the channel.

Drag popped up periodically throughout my childhood, and I was unusually lucky (especially for a kid growing up in a military context) that the circumstances were always positive. When I was a middle-schooler in the Canadian prairies, one of my dance teachers was a young gay man and nobody made negative comments, even when they heard that he dabbled in drag. Instead, they cheered when he choreographed a kids' jazz number to RuPaul's song 'Supermodel'. My mom's media consumption also continued to introduce me subtly to drag. I discovered Lady Bunny at the back of what my aunts referred to as 'trashy magazines': pop-culture rags filled with celebrity gossip. Bunny was a regular feature on the back two pages, once again providing scathing and witty fashion reviews of some of Hollywood's most outrageous get-ups.

I suppose it was no real surprise, then, when I grew up, realized my queerness and started doing drag myself. My mom has joked that between being dragged from posting to posting across the world and being *in* drag now, I didn't grow up – I was dragged up. A few short years after donning my first set of triple-stacked 301 false lashes, I was travelling the world with my best friend, cameras in hand as we obsessively documented as much drag, of as many different kinds, as humanly possible.

My initial exposure to drag was so positive that it hadn't prepared me for the backlash this art form can elicit, particularly for those who do not fit the mould of 'classic' cis male drag queen as portrayed or parodied in movies. Early in my drag career, I faced queerphobia from those outside the queer community, but also (much more unexpectedly) misogyny from *within* it for being a cis female drag queen. Evidently, what I did wasn't 'real' drag because of my gender and genitals; I was assumed to be straight and accused of

appropriating 'gay culture'. The backlash from drag traditionalists eventually threatened not only my bookings, but also my very safety in local drag spaces. Instead of giving up, however, I stubbornly pivoted; if they wouldn't let me on stage, I'd find other ways to participate in drag. I filmed all my friends doing it, assisted them at their gigs and broke into the production side of shows and tours. I adored drag for the way it helped me to reclaim my identity in the face of suffocating social norms, and I was determined to work in it regardless of what some men said. Through our drag media platform Drag Coven, that's exactly what I have done.

Ten years later I've had the privilege of experiencing drag globally. I've seen queens assist illusionists in sweaty basements in Poland, at a time when queerness was so politically threatened that I didn't even realize the personal risk my attendance involved until the performers thanked us profusely for our daring support. I've filmed queens from the Philippines as they ran around a dive bar in Los Angeles, lip-syncing duets while doing exhausting physical comedy like climbing the furniture and tossing a microphone back and forth in increasingly extravagant ways without ever missing a catch. I've worked press-week red carpets, lived on tour buses with reality stars and given a performer the bra right off my body to solve a costume malfunction (twice). The creativity, love and mutual support that I've experienced in drag have *always* outweighed the opposite.

The more I've travelled, the more aware I have become that drag is much more than glitz and glam. Those who never witness it outside their local bar or explore the artists who *haven't* appeared on their favourite television shows miss out on something beautifully intricate, historically informed and culturally impactful. I love the world's most recognizable drag stars as much as the next person, and indeed I'm fortunate to have built lasting friendships with people I'd previously only admired on the screen, but what about the foundation on which those careers are built? Even casual drag fans recognize the phrase 'know your herstory', but experience has taught me that it's really of a patchwork of herstories from across the globe. Where do the queens you've seen on

television really come from? What norms and traditions have influenced their drag evolution? How does that differ one city, one province, one state or one continent over? This is what *Planet Drag* explores.

DRAG: DRESSES AND DISRUPTION

Countercultures are an intrinsic part of the human experience. Niche groups develop parallel to the systems of power that organize our world and dictate how we navigate society – or, at least, how we're supposed to. Subcultures vary wildly and manifest through differing methods, tools and theories, but all share a similar central ethos: to disrupt the norm.

Which norm a group interrogates varies just as widely as their approach. The purpose of any successful counterculture is to uproot the central tenets of society that dominant groups accept without thought; to make us wonder *why* we do things the way we do, and if there might be a different (or better) way. That challenge can manifest as art, writing, performance, protest or music, and the range of mediums countercultures employ is constantly evolving.

Very few countercultures have as unique and stirring a combination of elements as drag. Drag performance is almost singular in its historical endurance, social impact and deeply transgressive nature. Wrap it all up in a multifaceted visual package that – depending on the artist – might entice or appal, amuse or disturb, empower or enrage. At the same time as drag provides participants with a platform on which to seek self-expression, connection and autonomy, it also intentionally puts one of life's

OPPOSITE: RuPaul Charles, the now-infamous 'supermodel of the world', in 1992. Before RuPaul became the host of *RuPaul's Drag Race* and changed the course of drag history, she wore many hats. She was a gender-bending club kid in the 1980s, a regular feature on daytime talk shows in the 1990s, a pop recording artist, and the first drag queen to be featured in a MAC Viva Glam makeup campaign. She even had her own show, *The RuPaul Show*, which first aired in 1996.

most inherent and fundamental concepts – gender – under a scathingly analytical microscope.

DRAG WHODUNIT

Most people have encountered drag in some popularized form. Perhaps you've seen a Hollywood film in which an actor dons a dress for comedic value. Maybe you've laughed at pantomimes as the 'dame' exaggerates stereotypical femininity for the purposes of light-hearted social commentary. If you're a fan of drag as an art form, you may even know the common myth that the term 'drag' originated as an acronym – Dressed Resembling A Girl – in the days of Shakespearean theatre, when female characters were played by male actors as the law prohibited women from performing on-stage in civilized society (see the chapter on the United Kingdom on pages 148–159).

At its heart, however, drag is a far more intersectional enigma than simply dressing up to resemble a girl, as it were. In fact, the claim that this is where the term originated, as though this act invented drag as we know it today, is a misconception – but more on that later. Drag's *authentic* history has fallen victim to erasure over time thanks to biased documentation (or, in some cases, a devastating lack of documentation), making drag's truly diverse origins a surprise to many.

Even the drag community itself, for a time, fell prey to binary understandings of what gender performance is, what it looks like and who typically does it. For decades, based on its limited representation in pop culture, drag was understood primarily as when a man (usually gay) dresses up as a woman for entertainment. Drag kings – stereotypically women who dress and perform as men – were a lesser-known entity, often brushed aside or included in drag discourse only as a footnote. Everyone else (and there are *countless* artists and identities in this category) is hardly acknowledged by drag's 'classic definition'. Periods of queer historical erasure falsely attributed drag's origins to cis gay men for many years. Of course, men have always broken down barriers and achieved great things in drag, but they were not the sole proprietors they're often asserted to be.

In reality, drag is widely understood by its most immersed and experienced participants as having originated with transgender women of colour. Drag as its own performance genre was never made up solely of drag queens but rather of queens, kings, showgirls, divas, drag things, gender-benders and countless other embodiments of gender performance. Local stories, word-of-mouth and personal accounts of drag history have long included non-binary people, butch lesbians, transgender men and agender individuals playing integral roles in global drag history alongside their gay male and transfemme counterparts. People of all identities perform as kings, queens and all kinds of transgressive characters in between.

The common thread of the drag world is not a definition of what it is or should be. Rather, it's the central aim to radicalize what we can *all* be if we free ourselves, even temporarily, from society's expectations and communicate our identities to the world in whichever way feels most authentic and fulfilling. Drag doesn't only seek to dislodge the idea that we 'should' look, feel, act, live and love in a certain way based on our assigned gender at birth. It also mocks and satirizes the very systems that seek to oppress not just queer individuals and bodies, but everyone. Drag is, at its heart, a queering of hegemony packaged in just enough glitz and glamour to tantalize, just enough filth and horror to shock, or just enough sultry sizzle to seduce its consumers into interrogating for themselves whether gender rules are really in our best interests.

OPPOSITE: The Boulet Brothers, chilling icons of Los Angeles drag, are the hosts of the hit series *Dragula*, a horror-based TV drag competition. Here, they pose with their 'Creatures of The Night' podcast co-host Ian DeVoglaer in Toronto.

SPOTLIGHT, SPOTLIGHT (BABY, COME ON)!

Drag, pop culture and mainstream entertainment have a long and cosy relationship, although not an altogether equitable one. In fact, half the trends we catch on to as mixed-media consumers – the lingo, style and mannerisms we absorb from our favourite actors, singers and other celebrities – have come from those celebrities' own exposure to counterculture artists. Drag performers have always been influencing pop divas and silver-screen sweethearts behind the scenes, putting their creative skills to good use for the benefit of wider entertainment; their names are simply afforded a lesser platform and therefore less public credit than their bigger bosom buddies. Of course, drag queens in particular are no stranger to screens, but their niche role is often short cameos and their constant competition is the trope of a recognizable leading man in a shake-and-go wig.

The age of reality television in the early 2000s, however, unwittingly set the stage for the drag industry's biggest shift yet towards the mainstream. The premiere in 2009 of *RuPaul's Drag Race*, an American competition show for performing drag queens, allowed drag as an art form to stick its heeled foot a little more firmly through the doors to Hollywood. Since then, the *Drag Race* franchise has skyrocketed to infamy, experiencing nothing but exponential growth for its sociocultural impact.

With the arrival on the scene of *Drag Race*, audiences and entertainers alike turned their attention to drag artists in unprecedented ways. Of course, *RuPaul's Drag Race* is not solely responsible for the presence of drag in the mainstream spotlight, but its unmitigated success and the subsequent popularity of other drag-centred series, such as *The Boulet Brothers' Dragula*, *Call Me Mother*, *Camp Wannakiki*, *The Switch*, *Queen of the Universe*, *Drag Den*, *Drag Me to Dinner* and *House of Drag New Zealand*, elevated the visibility of drag and its participants in a way that was nothing short of game-changing.

The success of televised drag has had a nuanced and complicated impact on the global drag scene, just as it would on any intricate subculture system –

particularly one that so many people still regard as contentious. It's undoubtedly true, however, that the longer drag television airs, the more the art form becomes normalized in new and previously inaccessible spaces, so that large-scale interest in and opportunities for drag artists grow.

The increased visibility of drag has fostered previously impossible collaborations, particularly due to the internet. Cities start networking groups for drag swaps, open stage calls and skill-sharing. There is a transaction of drag-based information, giving artists commonality. At the same time, wider cultural influences and personal experiences help scenes and individuals from different areas to maintain distinction. As drag thrives and performers see more opportunities to travel and connect, they learn new tricks, absorb phrases and mannerisms, and pass on tips. A contemporary cross-contamination fosters a unique balance between homogenization and increased diversity.

Although it's been only a short time in the grand scheme of drag's history, drag-related television has been airing for more than a decade now, generating new, young drag artists whose knowledge and conception of drag and all its facets are heavily affected by and often built on what they see on *RuPaul's Drag Race* and its counterparts. As such, some homogenization has unavoidably taken place. As phenomenal as drag's globalization is for those who both do and consume it, the *Drag Race*-ification of drag may have consequences for the industry as well. The longer *Drag Race* is on television, the more polished the contestants' packages become.

As the show's popularity has grown, its impact has spread ever wider. Recent seasons of many international versions of the show have featured young contestants speaking openly about previous *Drag Race* alumni being their idols, role models and greatest inspiration. It makes sense, then, that similarities between certain styles of costume, make-up or wig can be seen not just between show contestants, but also among performers in many different areas of the drag industry. The more drag artists consume one another's content, work together and travel to new places to perform, the more opportunity they have to influence one another's art. Of course, the transference of knowledge and style between practitioners of art and culture is not a negative thing, but this emerging reality does highlight the importance of learning about, showcasing and preserving the unique elements of drag's local scenes.

Perhaps the best example of how drag and the internet have become intrinsically intertwined was born out of the COVID-19 pandemic. When public queer spaces shut down the world over, many vulnerable communities found themselves not just isolated like everyone else, but completely cut off from people like them – except online. Suddenly drag's deep links to social media became a lifeline for connection rather than just a networking tool or a venue for 'drag drama' to thrive. Drag artists across the globe made even more headlines than usual for their innovation and leadership in digital entertainment, and this time it wasn't just the 'TV queens' who got recognition.

When the island of Newfoundland became the only place in Canada where it was legal to hold in-person shows, thanks to the prolonged protection from viral spread afforded by its remote location, mainlanders were patched in via livestreams to spread a little queer joy to those in isolation. Australian performers, on the other hand, found a unique way to keep performing in person, but from a safe distance; they drove to different neighbourhoods to do numbers at the ends of driveways while families watched from the porch. The ingenuity of this idea inspired artists internationally to set up socially distanced events in new places.

While such examples prove that drag and the internet can foster community, the unpleasant post-lockdown backlash spurred by the rise in right-wing confidence ignited by the COVID-19 anti-vaccination movement exemplifies the darker side of how drag is affected by the ways in which online spaces make queerness (and queer artists) more generally accessible. The United Kingdom and the United States (particularly southern states), for example, have been racked by calls for drag bans since the rise in popularity of drag story times, a long-standing, family-friendly phenomenon that conservatives caught wind of and took unkindly to when drag was forced to shift online during COVID-19 lockdowns.

Drag artists are now held up by the political right as a 'threat to children' and used as a tool by which people with queerphobic beliefs mask their desire to prevent primarily trans people from participating in public life. The higher drag's star rises, the more drag artists are exposed to the harmful pitfalls of celebrity, even if they've never appeared on a television series. The price of success is greater visibility, and drag's journey into the spotlight reminds us why representation is so important. Praise might equal price now, but no entertainer will forget that drag is, and always has been, political.

KNOW YOUR HERSTORY

Perhaps the most important facet of *Drag Race*'s global success has been its franchise expansion into the international sphere. With the development of televised drag platforms in Thailand, Canada, the UK, Holland, Italy, Spain, France, Mexico, Brazil, Sweden, Belgium and the Philippines, the magnified lens and creation of opportunity generated by its success reach a global scale. As such, the chance for drag-specific cultural crossover and the exchange of queer knowledge between local performers and audiences the world over has also been handed a remarkable new channel through which to flow.

As global drag becomes increasingly polished and standardized in many ways, the varied nature of its roots becomes especially valuable. This is perfectly displayed by the ways in which performers from Canada, New Zealand and the Philippines, for example, can all use their drag as a tool of decolonization without really overlapping in theme, even if the artists participate in similar contemporary style trends here and there. Seeking out local drag communities in the countries that are showcased on television becomes a practice in informing ourselves about different artists, their home scenes and the history of drag where they come from. This, in turn, feeds the wider drag industry and the cycle that has so far kept drag's current mainstream boom thriving.

After all, local drag scenes are the talent pool from which our favourite drag television shows are cast. Where do the artists we love to see at viewing parties come from? What cultural nuances and lived experiences inform the way their drag has evolved? How can we see the customs and sociopolitical influences from which their home scene grew in what they bring to our screens? *Planet Drag* teases out the unique ways in which different countries across the world have transgressed gender, fought against hegemony and woven fabrics of queer experience over time.

The better international drag scenes are supported, the more opportunity and income the artists are afforded, and the better prepared they'll be to work on an international scale, whether on television or elsewhere. Artists who are properly compensated for their work before they hit the screen may spend more time, thought and intentionality putting their package together, increasing their potential for learning about and incorporating elements of their home scene's style and culture. The chain reaction continues when young viewers see themselves represented either on-screen or onstage, in terms of not just queerness but also local context and influence. In the following chapters, queer writers and drag artists from different parts of the world delve into the interwoven relationships between history, politics, identity and artistic expression to explore how drag has not only been shaped by but has also shaped so many countries' entertainment spheres in ways that are not always made apparent on our favourite television shows.

Unless you have the unique privilege of being a world traveller, the process of learning about niche cultures across the world is heavily affected by the accessibility of information, and endangered by the concept of erasure or selective archiving. A perk of drag's current heightened visibility, however, is that contemporary drag of every kind, and at every level, is being documented more effectively than ever before.

Even better, queer historians are delving into drag's history, retrieving information, names and stories that deserve to be preserved and known. The emphasis on grass-roots support and local histories begins the process of more authentically capturing drag's truly diverse nature, as well as the reality that all kinds of people have always done all types of drag. Long before 'The Queen of Drag' was arrested for throwing an all-drag birthday party in 1888, women famously performed as men in Tang Dynasty Chinese opera in about the year 618. It is my humble hope that Planet Drag will play a role in helping people to learn even more about drag's true and very global nature. The aim is for the book to be a puzzle piece in the pivotal process of patchworking together wider drag histories. If there's one thing I've learned from a decade of building Drag Coven's diverse archive, it's that the most exciting drag can be found where you least expect it. Even the smallest shows, the littlest scenes and the quietest artists can shift mountains when it comes to queer activism and community-building. Without the local leaders and global trailblazers of old, our favourite shows would not exist today. Planet Drag maps out drag's quirks and variations, inspirations and cultural influences, formats and formulas across the planet, with consideration for places that have yet to join the franchised empire. If we take the time to look at what is in front of and around us, I firmly believe that queer people and our allies will forge ahead more prepared and inspired than ever before.

NOTE TO READER

The language surrounding sexual and gender identity is constantly shifting and evolving and the utmost care and attention has been made over pronouns in every case in this book. We would apologise in advance for any errors, and will make any amendments for any reprints if notified in writing.

BEYOND PRISCILLA, HERE IS THE FORMER 'DRAG CAPITAL OF THE WORLD'

Courtney Norton

For most readers, the words 'Australian drag' probably bring to mind the bold make-up and foam wigs of the film *The Adventures of Priscilla, Queen of the Desert* (1994). The kooky, entertaining classic was undeniably influential, but there's much more to drag down under. Dig deep and you'll find a rich, surprising, subversive history, rooted in wicked humour and a distinctly Aussie desire to 'give anything a go'. There's a reason that, according to LitHub, Sydney was the 1960s 'drag capital of the world', so buckle up as we delve deep into the country's wildly under-represented drag history.

DRAG AND POLITICS

Although not affiliated with specific political parties, Australian drag performers have always prided themselves on advocating for the voiceless. It's not unusual for performances to tackle heavy issues, such as race, gender, class and sexuality, and in a persuasive thesis in 2012, the scholar of psychology and public health Ronald Del Castillo even described drag as an extension of the country's sexual liberation movement.

There are early reports of cross-dressing in Australia's criminal records, but it wasn't until the 1920s that a true drag subculture began to bubble up. In elaborate balls held across Sydney – events that weren't specifically gay, but more generally 'bohemian' – partygoers could drag up in relative safety, performing in decadent costumes to crowds of eager onlookers. By the 1950s these balls had become annual, hugely popular extravaganzas.

In common with most countries, Australia had harsh laws against homosexuality and cross-dressing until the late twentieth century. In the southern island state of Tasmania, same-sex activity wasn't decriminalized until 1997, more than two decades later than in the rest of the country. Yet such laws couldn't stop drag from thriving; in the 1960s, in particular, within just a few years drag bars such as Les Girls, Jewel Box and the Purple Onion emerged across Sydney, each advertising drag performers to eager, mixed crowds.

The Purple Onion was known for platforming the chaotic, gloriously punk drag of Sylvia and the Synthetics, a sprawling artist collective formed in 1972. Their performances were 'more Iggy Pop punk rock than Les Girls showgirls', according to *The Guardian*, and it wasn't unusual for crowds to leave covered in whipped cream, fake blood or dead fish. The Synthetics' favoured aesthetic was rooted in gender-bending; think leg hair poking through ripped fishnets, finished with cheap stilettos.

It has increasingly been acknowledged that as AIDS spread through Australia in the 1980s, drag performers were on the front line of protests advocating for healthcare. The series *In Our Blood* (2023) provides a dramatized retelling of the community's response to the virus in Australia, and it features drag performers front and centre. Yet these histories are often erased, so the work of piecing them together is ongoing.

More recently, as in many other countries, drag performers in Australia have faced a backlash for hosting youth-focused events. This extends beyond concerned criticism, to encompass real threats of physical violence and doxing. Thankfully, in what was perhaps a pleasant surprise, some politicians not only condemned those violent actions, but also outwardly supported such events as Drag Queen Story Hour. In fact, Victoria's state Parliament House hosted its very own drag-queen story session, held on the International Day against Homophobia, Biphobia and Transphobia in May 2023. Among those in attendance was state premier Daniel Andrews, who asked the protestors: 'What are you protesting against? You're just

> "Times have changed immeasurably since the decriminalization of homosexuality, yet even now, it's drag performers who are leading the fight for lasting social change."

using it as a platform for your vile hatred. It's awful. If you don't want to go to these events, don't go.'

There's still much to be done in terms of LGBTQ+ equality in Australia, but seeing politicians step forward and support drag performers openly is a promising sign of progress to come. Times have changed immeasurably since the decriminalization of homosexuality, yet even now, it is drag performers who are leading the fight for lasting social change.

AUSTRALIA'S DRAG OSCARS

For decades, Australian drag communities have been celebrated at the annual DIVAs, the Drag Industry Variety Awards. The ceremony is a guaranteed hot ticket: think all the glitz, glamour and drama of the Oscars, but with *far* more camp.

This tradition dates back to 1990, when the glitter-soaked, gloriously foul-mouthed Cindy Pastel won the award for Entertainer of the Year. In 1991 Sydney's DCM nightclub amped up the glamour by holding the first ever in-person iteration of the awards ceremony, and since then, the DIVAs have become an Australian drag institution. The categories are tongue-in-cheek – for years, the top honour was 'Bitch of the Year' – but

ABOVE: Drag performer standing tall as part of a protest supporting marriage equality.

they are also wide-ranging, designed to showcase venues, collectives and queer community initiatives.

These awards are prestigious, and they often give a glimpse into the future of Australian drag. When *RuPaul's Drag Race* launched its Down Under edition in 2021, it came as no surprise to see former DIVA winners, such as Maxi Shield and Coco Jumbo, on the line-up, as well as Minnie Cooper – who won Miss Rising Star in 2004, before consistently sweeping the top categories in later years – in Season 2.

Then, of course, there's Courtney Act, who was first crowned Miss Rising Star back in 2002 and even now remains the first name that comes to mind when Australians are asked to name a famous drag queen. Her blonde bombshell beauty, impressive vocals and bubbly personality have made her an icon, not just within Australia's drag community, but for the country in general. To call her a reality TV pioneer would be no understatement.

After rising through the ranks of Australia's drag scene, in 2003 Courtney became the first drag performer in the history of *Australian Idol*, winning over the public and earning a recording contract with BMG Australia (now Sony Music Australia) later that year. Her debut single, 'Rub Me Wrong', peaked at number 29 on the ARIA Singles Chart and earned gold certification. Whether or not she knew it at the time, her appearance on *Australian Idol* was the start of many firsts, not just for Courtney but also for popular culture in general. These include being the first drag artist to appear on Australian reality TV as a contestant, the first drag artist to debut on a major record label globally, and the first out queer contestant on any *Idol* franchise in the world. In an interview for *Australian Story*, Courtney explained that she believed it was *Idol* judge Ian 'Dicko' Dickson's celebration of her that was 'instrumental and fundamental' to mainstream Australia's acceptance of her.

Courtney's position as a recognizable face on television meant that many Australians were seeing drag for the first time, and her influence on members of the country's drag scenes both new and old is undeniable. Thanks in no small part to Courtney and her high-femme beat, Australian drag make-up in the early to mid-2000s shifted towards a style of 'feminine illusion'. Since then she has cemented herself as a force to be reckoned with, an Australian drag talent known around the world.

AUSTRALIAN DRAG ON-SCREEN

"Courtney [Act]'s position as a reconizable face on television meant that many Australians were seeing drag for the first time, and her influence on members of the country's drag scenes is undeniable."

It's a brilliantly slapstick premise: two drag queens and a trans woman embark on a chaotic low-budget trip across Australia, their rickety pink-and-lavender bus chugging along under the weight of hot-glued costumes. This is the plot of *The Adventures of Priscilla, Queen of the Desert*, which was responsible for catapulting Australian drag into the global mainstream.

First, a few disclaimers. None of the performers was *actually* a drag queen. The three leading roles went to Hugo Weaving, Guy Pearce and Terence Stamp, well-known actors chosen to lure mainstream viewers into the improbable story of a ragtag drag troupe. The wigs and headpieces were gravity-defying and the costumes delightfully garish and dripping with sequins – so much so that the film's costume designers, Lizzy Gardiner and Tim Chappel, won an Academy Award for their work in 1995.

What makes this success even more impressive is that *Priscilla* was made on a low budget – at least by Hollywood standards – meaning the cast and crew had to get creative. Take the show-stopping performance at an Alice Springs casino, for example. The scene featured breathtaking costumes designed to mimic the evolutionary cycle, and the *pièce de résistance* is a beautiful gown made from crystal organza. According to an article in *The Guardian*, the look required 150 pom-poms – a tall order for the costume department – so construction was outsourced to inmates

of Long Bay prison in Malabar, New South Wales, under the strict condition that the prisoners should not be allowed scissors. Another famous look is the so-called thong dress, adorned with the strappy beach sandals commonly known elsewhere as flip-flops. Although it was iconic, Chappel revealed to *ABC News* that the dress cost about $17 in total to construct, using thongs and hot glue bought from Target. The reason? His mum worked there, and could get them a 15 per cent discount.

Beyond the glamour and hilarious one-liners – who could forget the immortal 'cock in a frock' quip? – the film has real heart, and it had a huge sociocultural impact on Australia. Weaving later said that *Priscilla* shone a light on the Australian perspective of what it meant to be 'a man', and that through it, boundaries of Australian masculinity were essentially 'thrown out the window'. The film's success had a ripple effect on Australian drag, pulling it more firmly into the mainstream and influencing drag performers to be more bold, ballsy and over-the-top than ever before.

Rumour has it that the film was inspired by real-life Australian performers. In her official website biography, the famous showgirl Carlotta describes herself as one of the inspirations behind *Priscilla*, although there's little mention of this elsewhere online. Although not strictly a drag performer, Carlotta is a trailblazer in her own right. In 1959 she became a leading showgirl at Sydney's Les Girls cabaret bar, enrapturing audiences with her wicked sense of humour and glamorous, high-femme looks.

ABOVE: One of the most iconic shots from *The Adventures of Priscilla, Queen of the Desert*.

OPPOSITE: Australian trans icon, Carlotta.

She broke new ground as a trans starlet, quickly cementing her status as the main attraction of Les Girls' roster, and fans loved her so much that they took to calling her 'Carlotta, Queen of the Cross'. Soon afterwards, mainstream television came knocking, and in 1973 she made history by becoming the first trans actor to play a trans character, in the soap opera *Number 96*.

Even before *Priscilla*, there was a history of drag on-screen in Australia, most notably in the form of Dame Edna Everage, the drag alter ego of the comedian Barry Humphries. A satirical send-up of an elderly suburban housewife, Dame Edna made her way into homes worldwide and reigned supreme in the entertainment industry for decades. Yet her legacy was tarnished in 2018, when Humphries came under fire for describing transness as a 'fashion'.

By contrast, *Priscilla* has long been viewed more fondly by drag fans worldwide. Even now, drag performers across Australia and beyond have created their own tributes to the film through themed shows, re-creating costumes and quoting the lines in hilarious monologues, screaming: 'That's it, no more fucking ABBA!' Yet one of *Priscilla*'s best-known quotations nods to the beating heart beyond the comedy. 'I can only fight because I've learned to,' says Bernadette, in a moment of uncharacteristic earnestness. 'Being a man one day and a woman the next isn't an easy thing to do.'

SYDNEY GAY AND LESBIAN MARDI GRAS

In 1978, after receiving a letter from San Francisco activists requesting acts of solidarity for the anniversary of the Stonewall riots and their march against the anti-gay Briggs Initiative in California (which sought to ban gay people from working in schools), Ken Davis and Annie Talve brought together a group of people who eventually became known as the Gay Solidarity Group. On the evening of 24 June 1978 the Gay Solidarity Group and its supporters gathered on Oxford Street in Sydney – the city's 'gay strip' – dancing and celebrating as they marched towards Hyde Park. Among them was the drag queen Trixie Le Bon, who encouraged others to join them along the way.

Despite approving a permit for the march, police began to rush at the revellers, many of whom were beaten, handled violently and thrown into the back of patrol cars. The only float present that day was confiscated. Yet – much in the spirit of the Stonewall riots (see the United States chapter on pages 172–183)– the crowd fought back, and fifty-three people were charged at Darlinghurst police station.

Davis, who recalls hearing marchers in the police station being beaten and crying out in pain, describes the night as having gone from 'nerve-wracking to exhilarating to traumatic all in the space of a few hours'.

He said, however, that this only made them more determined to run Mardi Gras again the following year.

While there have been sincere attempts to repair the Mardi Gras celebration's relationship with the police, it has remained complicated in the years since. Those who were there that very first year have become known as the '78ers' and have featured in every Mardi Gras parade since, attracting some of the loudest cheers of the event. More than four decades on, the parade is bigger than ever, with over 500,000 parade attendees and more than 10,000 marchers (with drag performers among them, of course) every year. It's a high-camp extravaganza, and although billed as the 'Gay and Lesbian Mardi Gras', it has, over the years, made an effort to be inclusive of the entire LGBTQ+ community.

For drag performers, Mardi Gras is the Super Bowl, a month-long celebration culminating in the world-famous parade on the first Saturday in March. From high camp to high glamour and everything in between, you can find events for just about every type of drag, with the range only increasing every year. In fact, you'd be hard-pressed to find a style of drag that *isn't* represented at Mardi Gras.

As with similar events worldwide, the roots of Sydney's Mardi Gras are in protest and resistance. Amid the elaborate costumes and cheeky, hilarious drag performances, there's a sense of rebelliousness and resilience that continues to define LGBTQ+ communities and the art of drag worldwide. It's a beautiful spectacle, one that celebrates drag excellence across Australia and lures tourists from around the world, all keen to soak in the euphoria of this spectacular event.

DRAG AND INDIGENOUS CULTURE

> "The celebration of culture and the uplifting of Aboriginal and Torres Strait Islander individuals, and the excavation and preservation of their histories, are essential."

It's not uncommon for Indigenous cultures worldwide to have rich, expansive conceptions of gender, which stretch way beyond the 'male/female' binary that has until recently been seen as fixed in Western societies. The Torres Strait Islanders of Australia are no exception. Whether it's gender expression through art and performance or in day-to-day life, or a combination of the two, Indigenous Australians exemplify the fluidity of gender in a uniquely beautiful and honest fashion.

This is prominent in the Sistergirl community. 'Sistergirl' is a term used by Aboriginal and Torres Strait Islander people to describe gender-diverse people with a female spirit, or who take on feminine roles within their communities. Crystal Love, affectionately known as 'the aunty of the Sistergirl community', is an icon for Sistergirls and Brotherboys, as well as for Indigenous Australians and for those in the country's drag community more generally.

Crystal's community work extends from being a mentor to the Yimpininni (a group of Sistergirls in the Tiwi Islands) to Australia-wide causes, such as the referendum for an Indigenous voice to parliament in 2023. She frequently uses her platform as a well-known performer to elevate and amplify voices that are all too often unheard, and in doing so, she has become a role model for drag performers across Australia. Her excellence was even formally recognized in 2023, when she won the Rainbow Champion Award at Sydney's World Pride.

In a community that still has a great deal of healing to do as a result of colonization, the celebration of culture and the uplifting of Aboriginal and Torres Strait Islander individuals, and the excavation and preservation of their histories, are essential. In the drag community, this comes in the form of the 'Miss First Nation Pageant', a glamorous showcase of Indigenous drag excellence. The importance of this event can't be understated. In an interview with *Creative Spirits*, Timberlina – a finalist in 2018 – explained its huge impact on Australia's drag scene. 'There were no Aboriginal Torres Strait Islander drag queens out there,' she said. 'And now, they're all coming out of the woodwork, which is amazing. It's because of this competition. Words can't explain how amazing it is.' All too often, drag is described in a Western context only, but there's an

OPPOSITE: Courtney Act attends the 3rd Annual *RuPaul's DragCon LA* in 2017.

BELOW: Timberlina, a finalist in the 2018 Miss First Nation Pageant.

extensive lineage of gender-based performance in Indigenous, pre-colonial societies, and it is finally being recognized.

One such example is performer Miss Ellaneous, a descendant of the Iwaidja and Malak Malak clans, and the people of Badu Island on the Torres Strait Islands; in an interview with *NITV News*, she beautifully summarized the natural affinity between drag and Australian Indigenous cultures. 'We come from the oldest surviving culture on the planet,' she explained, 'so we've got music, storytelling, song and dance in our DNA. I think that's what makes us unique as performers and artists and drag queens, that knowledge and culture.'

RADICAL DRAG, COFFEE LOUNGE CRUISING AND MĀORI PERFORMANCE

Courtney Norton

Because New Zealand is tucked away in a quiet corner of the world, it might not be the first place that comes to mind when you think of iconic drag scenes. Its drag scene is certainly small, but it sure is mighty – and arguably for this reason deserves a bigger share of the global spotlight.

NEW ZEALAND'S DRAG BEGINNINGS

It's now widely acknowledged that drag is about gender expression and experimentation; it's not mere cross-dressing, but rather about creating beautiful displays of heightened gender performance. New Zealand's LGBTQ+ advocates were early adopters of such progressive thinking. In the July 1973 edition of the Christchurch Gay Liberation Front newsletter, Lindsay Taylor presented a definition of drag that challenged what it meant to be 'a man':

> *An example of radical drag is a man who wears female clothes but who also wears a beard … he's not trying to act like a woman. He's showing that clothes and behaviour have no relations to a person's essential masculinity or femininity; he's showing that our attitudes to masculinity and femininity are conditioned by what society has taught us to believe, and not by what we really are.*

This gives a glimpse into the disruptive, gender-bending drag scene of New Zealand, which dates back at least to the 1950s. Early shows were firmly underground to ensure the safety of both participants and audience, and event details were disclosed solely on a 'need to know' basis. In his book *Mates and Lovers* (2008), Chris Brickell describes the 1970s as a turning point, an era in which drag really 'jumped off the stage and into the streets' – at least in the big cities, such as Auckland and Wellington.

The drag icon Johnny Croskery played a key role in cementing these years as New Zealand drag's heyday. Throughout the 1960s he performed in iconic venues in Wellington, including Carmen's International Coffee Lounge and Carmen's Balcony Strip Club, flaunting the towering orange wigs and glamorous aesthetic that soon became his signature. In the Balcony, Croskery performed as half of the legendary cabaret duo Frankie and Johnny, taking the 1970s by storm.

Croskery looks back fondly on the openness of Wellington at the time. In an early interview, reprinted in *Mates and Lovers*, he recalls that many of the men he knew on the ships from England loved coming to the city. 'They used to bring all of their clothes, and we used to go out on the town while they were here, hop into drag and go out to restaurants, and coffee shops and pubs,' he explained. 'There was nothing like this overseas, even in London. People used to go shopping in the daytime in drag, it was so open. Wellingtonians didn't bat an eyelid when they saw a drag queen sailing up Cuba Street in full regalia.'

It's noteworthy that 'drag' took on an expanded meaning in the 1970s, as part of the country's queer liberation movement. During the annual Gay Liberation Conference held at Victoria University in Wellington in 1974, the word was used as an all-inclusive term for those participating in and supported by the Gay Liberation Front, and it was made clear that

PREVIOUS PAGE: Kita Mean, the 'Queen of Camp' known for her bold, fun and eye-catching style.

OPPOSITE: New Zealand drag icon, Johnny Croskery, from his personal 1980s–1990s photo album.

this included LGBTQ+ people faced with additional oppression, such as 'women, Māoris [sic], Pacific Islanders, transvestites and trans-sexuals and blatant gays'. These marginalized communities were encouraged to form subgroups in order to give voice to topics that were of special significance to them.

The role played by trans women – especially *whakawāhine*, Māori trans women – in the 1970s liberation movement is increasingly being acknowledged. In an interview with *The Spinoff* in 2022, the activist Sandy Gauntlett underlined the fact that *whakawāhine* were 'community matriarchs who ran and staffed the coffee lounges, bars and night-time venues where the seeds of gay liberation germinated', and that although the official line was one of trans-inclusivity, Gauntlett and other trans activists were sometimes left wondering 'whether the gays wanted them'.

Such histories are always subject to interpretation, but New Zealand's queer liberation activists did push for trans-inclusivity, creating a friendly, accepting attitude that has defined the country's drag since its earliest days and is still prevalent today. In an interview with the *Sydney Morning Herald* in 2022, the Kiwi drag icon Spankie Jackzon summarized this spirit beautifully. 'We don't have everything in New Zealand,' she says, 'but … we have the most incredibly kind, loving, welcoming people. And I think that's what screams through our drag.'

"New Zealand's queer liberation activists did push for trans-inclusivity, creating a friendly, accepting attitude that has defined the country's drag since its earliest days and is still prevalent today."

Kiwi
Carmen
1960

DRAG ROYALTY

Nothing short of a community trailblazer, Carmen Rupe was a transgender Māori woman, entertainer, sex worker and activist. She opened a number of businesses that were perceived as scandalous, most famously Carmen's International Coffee House, which she founded in Wellington in 1967. In an interview for the Museum of New Zealand, she recalls buying the venue with money inherited from her grandfather, and immediately painting the walls an opulent red, adding purple carpets and black leather furniture. Rupe specifically hired LGBTQ+ staff, including plenty of drag queens. 'I dressed up as a madam, a classy madam, tits hanging out and split dresses,' she quips. 'All the drag queens I had working for me were very, very stunning and beautiful. They used to wear a lot of wigs, a lot of make-up and lovely miniskirts or split dresses and low-top dresses, because a lot of my girls had to have their busts done in Cairo.'

Rupe succeeded in creating a safe space for the LGBTQ+ community, sex workers and entertainers, who needed somewhere that they felt welcome. The lounge was a covert cruising spot, too, where coffee cups in different colours were used to indicate discreetly whether someone was straight, gay or interested in hooking up with a drag queen.

None of this had happened overnight for Rupe, who was already a beloved figure within the LGBTQ+ community when the lounge officially opened. In the late 1950s she worked briefly as a nurse before moving on to waiting tables. By night, she worked as both a drag performer and a sex worker in Kings Cross, Sydney.

As the queer liberation movement accelerated in the 1970s, Rupe took to the streets, participating fearlessly in countless protests and public initiatives. She took a punchy, tongue-in-cheek approach to activism, best exemplified by her bid for Mayor of Wellington in 1977, for which she chose a deliberately provocative slogan: 'Get in behind!' Naturally, Rupe had the policy proposals to back up her mayoral attempt; not only did she call for the decriminalization of sex work, but also she proposed lowering the drinking age and decriminalizing abortion. Although she didn't win, her mayoral run has been labelled by some as her most remarkable public performance.

In 1979 Rupe sold her businesses in Wellington and moved to Sydney, where she spent the rest of her life. By this point, she was so beloved that her friends held a farewell ball for about 300 guests at Wellington's Majestic Cabaret. Fittingly, on that jubilant evening she was crowned 'Queen of Wellington' and gifted a specially created *korowai* (cloak), a symbol of sartorial elegance truly fit for New Zealand's drag royalty.

Iconic status isn't reserved for drag queens, however. There's plenty of room for kings too, such as the Christchurch-born Hugo Grrrl. Hugo made his start in Wellington – and as featured in the documentary

ABOVE: Community trailblazer and trans icon, Carmen Rupe.

OPPOSITE: Drag king Hugo Grrrl.

The Man Behind the King (2019), he describes it as a hugely creative and inclusive city, one that he's proud of. 'I'm led to believe that we don't face nearly as much of the gatekeeping and prejudice and straight-up misogyny that happens in a lot of other cities and communities,' he explains. 'Drag kings have existed in this community for a long time … Wellington does diversity pretty well on a global scale.'

Hugo isn't the country's only well-known drag king. Throughout the 1990s, the comedy duo the Topp Twins toured the country as their alter egos Ken and Ken, tongue-in-cheek send-ups of New Zealand farmers. With their brand of charismatic stand-up they earned the title of national treasures.

Hugo is continuing this legacy. As both a trans man and a drag king, he represents communities that are only too often denied the visibility they deserve. In the last few years alone, he has made huge strides in redressing this imbalance. In 2016 he created his well-known shows *Naked Girls Reading* and *The Pun Battle*, both of which were so successful that they resulted in tours across New Zealand.

It didn't take long for Hugo to earn serious credibility, and he appeared in the first series of the reality show *House of Drag* in 2018. Despite being the only drag king in the line-up – and the first drag king ever to appear on mainstream reality television – he earned the top spot with his wit, creativity and charisma, as well as a $10,000 prize. The victory opened eyes worldwide to his talent, and cemented his position as New Zealand's ultimate drag star.

Finally, you'd be hard pressed to find a drag performer with a bigger smile and bubblier personality than New Zealand's own Kita Mean. In common with many drag performers, Kita's first foray into drag was for a New Year's Eve party. What was intended as a one-night-only look quickly spiralled, and before long she was madly in love with drag, dedicating her time to polishing her skills.

Kita has been labelled the 'Queen of Camp', and this is a highly accurate, hard-earned moniker. When it comes to her drag looks, the brighter, the better. Patterns are bold, fun and eye-catching. Her aesthetic is the true embodiment of the 'more is more' rule, and it works. This bright, effervescent style is perfectly in step with her personality. Whether hosting a night at the world-famous Caluzzi's Cabaret, competing on television or simply interacting with audiences, her warmth and friendliness are obvious. In this sense, she's a quintessentially Kiwi performer, representing a culture that is known worldwide for its congeniality and openness.

Kita has worked hard for years to establish events across Auckland, but she was catapulted into the international spotlight back in 2018, when she hosted *House of Drag* alongside her fellow drag artist extraordinaire Anita Wigl'it. You may also recognize Kita as the first ever winner of *RuPaul's Drag Race Down Under*, which aired in 2021, a victory that confirmed her status as New Zealand's true Queen of Camp, a drag powerhouse worthy of international recognition.

ABOVE: Carmen Rupe's campaign poster during her run for Mayor of Wellington.

OPPOSITE: Drag queens Maude Boate, Anita Wigl'it and Kita Mean en route to the annual Broken Heel festival, paying homage to the iconic Australian film *The Adventures of Priscilla, Queen of the Desert.*

FA'AFAFINE

> "[Kita Mean] is a quintessentially Kiwi performer, representing a culture that is known worldwide for its congeniality and openness."

New Zealand may be small, but it's home to more than a dozen Indigenous communities, many of which have their own expansive views of gender. In Samoa, *fa'afafine* – which means 'in the way of a woman' – is a legally recognized third gender. Its best-known representative is Edward Cowley, a New Zealand-Samoan entertainer and activist also known as Buckwheat, a drag diva with a heart of gold.

Buckwheat was born in the 1990s in the Staircase, one of the earliest gay nightclubs in Auckland. Cowley had fallen in love with the club as a teenager, and later volunteered to transform himself into a drag hostess after a few other queens tried and failed to hold down the role. 'I realized I had to do it myself,' he recalled in 2022 in an interview with *Cityscape*. Despite the costume jewellery and polished, high-femme aesthetic, Buckwheat has never been the type of queen to insult her audiences.

Instead, Cowley says, she's 'really joyous and welcoming', with an eye to 'create mayhem, and welcome people, and give them a spectacle to look at'.

As well as polishing his drag, Cowley has spent his life advocating tirelessly for communities living with HIV, highlighting healthcare inequality and campaigning for the fair treatment of Pacific Islanders. Buckwheat remains a regular fixture at Auckland's annual Rainbow Pride Parades, and an endless source of inspiration for other *fa'afafine* performers rising through the ranks of drag both in New Zealand and in Samoa.

MĀORI CULTURE AND DRAG

It's impossible to discuss the role of Māori culture in New Zealand's drag scene without highlighting *irawhiti*, a te reo Māori word for people born with the spirit of a gender different from the one they were assigned at birth. It's an umbrella term that is used by trans women, trans men and non-binary people. *Ira kore* is the te reo Māori term used by people who don't identify with any gender at all. Historically, these communities have acted as passionate advocates for New Zealand's broader LGBTQ+ community, making invaluable contributions to the ongoing fight for liberation.

Perhaps the best-known recent example of Māori culture showcased through drag came as part of Sydney's World Pride 2023 celebrations. The proud Māori performer Aunty Tamara performed a *haka*, a ceremonial war dance or challenge intended to represent a group's pride, strength and unity. To the crowd's delight, onlookers joined in to create a truly memorable moment. Naturally, Tamara was met with thunderous applause.

Aunty Tamara later shared the video to her TikTok account, adding an impassioned caption that expressed her pride in Māori culture. 'This *haka* is a love letter and dedication to all POC, First Nation and Pacifica LGBTQIA+ people,' she wrote. 'This is something that breathes fire to my soul and something I hope to pass on to you all. To me, there is nothing more important than identity; knowing who you are as a person; and standing TALL, PROUD and UNAPOLOGETIC in everything you are.'

This wasn't the first time Aunty Tamara had recognized a space for connection between drag and Māori culture. In an interview with *Star Observer* in 2023, she described growing up with 'a background of cultural performing', which nurtured within her a 'deep passion' for Māori performance. 'To my surprise … this was not commonly seen in the drag scene – the cross-over between drag and Māori culture being performed,' she explained. 'To me, it was not that significant, but to others, it seemed to have a huge impact and [to] show an important point-of-view and perspective for Māori representation.'

Aunty Tamara's approach to fusing these two worlds is innovative, tongue-in-cheek and delightfully camp. In some performances, she uses *poi* – te reo Māori for 'ball on a cord', a traditional Māori performance object

– as part of her choreography, swinging it in rhythmic and geometric patterns. Only, in her hands, it's incorporated into high-octane routines soundtracked by such camp classics as 'It's Raining Men' and 'Stand Up'.

The importance of such crossovers can't be understated. When Māori drag performers incorporate traditional elements, such as *haka* and *poi*, into their performances, they're showing deep reverence for Māori culture *and* creating much-needed representation along the way.

Small but mighty. Passionate and strong. Creative and beautiful. New Zealand exemplifies all of these qualities both in their country overall as well as their drag performance scene. As the global drag spotlight expands even further, there's plenty of room for New Zealand to shine on an international scale.

"When Māori drag performers incorporate traditional elements into their performances, they're showing deep reverence for Māori culture and creating much-needed representation."

LAND OF THE RISING ILLUSIONISTS, WATERTRADE WORKERS, AND DRAG QUEENS WEIRD AND POP

Kat Joplin

Japan has a way of generating energy and excitement to an extent many times its size, and drag is no different. You might travel the world without finding a drag scene with as much diversity, innovation and intense emotion per square kilometre as that found in Japan. This is a place of many influences: foreign and Indigenous, pop and indie, occasionally angry and political. And it is a place that is changing and growing rapidly, and still in the process of making sense of itself.

Drag-queen styles in Japan vary widely by region and city, as well as according to cultural heritage and generation. The regal old-school glamour queens of some of Nagoya's bars are very different from the lively Brazilian–Japanese queens dancing just down the street. Kyoto is famous for its avant-garde performance artists, but just thirty minutes away, the Osaka bar-mamas are carousing with patrons and making everyone laugh until beer shoots from their noses. From Sapporo in the northernmost prefecture of Hokkaido to Naha in the southernmost islands of Okinawa, every major city (as well as a few rural hotspots) has its own distinct brand of drag and queer community. There really is something for everyone in the grand patchwork of Japanese drag.

CROSS-DRESSING AND CROSS-GENDER ACTING IN NOH, KYŌGEN, KABUKI AND THE TAKARAZUKA REVUE

Like most cultures around the world, Japan has had its fair share of historical cross-dressing performance and entertainment. Famous trickster heroes, such as Benten the Thief, were said to don women's costumes during their exploits; priests and male courtiers wore women's clothes and hairstyles at lavish parties; Heian novels tell tales of brothers and sisters swapped at birth; and shrine dancers (both male and female) dress as the opposite sex for festivals. One of the best examples of proto-drag in Japan are the Tekomai geisha of the Yoshiwara pleasure quarter of medieval Edo (now Tokyo). These geisha were much like drag kings today, and would dress as men to perform lion dances and plays to entertain the screaming crowds at festivals.

The most famous examples of cross-dressing on stage (cross-gender acting) in Japan belong to the institutions of Noh, kyōgen, kabuki and the Takarazuka Revue. Noh theatre and its comedic sister, kyōgen, developed in the fourteenth century, featuring actors sombrely chanting and slowly dancing, occasionally wearing masks to represent fantastical entities. Much as with Shakespearian theatre, women were banned from performing in Noh and kyōgen to preserve public morals, and female impersonation became the norm among male actors.

Kabuki launched in 1603 as a space for the common folk, bored of highbrow Noh performances, to enjoy wild costumes, raucous plays and intense action. By 1629 women had been banned from these stages as well, giving rise to the famous *onna-gata*, or male actresses, of kabuki theatre. Kabuki actors dress in robes of the Heian or Edo period, wear thick paint on their faces and hands, and don elaborate wigs. The most famous *onna-gata* are said to cast the female illusion perfectly through the exaggerated femininity of their body language.

As a further response to both all-male kabuki and all-male Noh-kyōgen, the all-female Takarazuka Revue emerged in 1914 as the

ABOVE: Takarazuka Revue, all-female musical productions, where performers resemble both drag kings and queens.

OPPOSITE: An *onnagata* ('woman's manner'), an actor in Kabuki theatre who plays female characters. While they are popularly considered one of Japan's indigenous drag queen counterparts, it should be noted that kabuki today does not consider itself queer, and often pressures queer actors to keep their indentities a secret.

brainchild of Ichizo Kobayashi, president of Hankyu railway company. The actors of Takarazuka play both female (*musumeyaku*) and male (*otokoyaku*) roles in flamboyant, typically Western-style musicals. With their wigs, sparkling costumes and dramatic make-up, the *musumeyaku* and *otokoyaku* strongly resemble today's drag queens and kings.

Because they prominently feature cross-gender acting, these traditions – in particular kabuki and Takarazuka – are often perceived by Westerners as 'Japan's version of drag', much to the chagrin of Japan's actual drag scene. It is important to remember that, despite the striking gender illusion on stage, these are conservative cisgender-heterosexual male-controlled institutions that do not officially associate with queerness (although, certainly, they have always involved some privately queer actors, as well as numerous queer fans). These theatres are not considered by most to be drag in the usual sense, but they are an important part of the conversation about gender studies in East Asia, and have influenced the drag queens and kings of Japan and the wider world.

DANSHŌ, GEI BŌI AND THE FIRST JAPANESE DRAG QUEENS

The true queens of Japan originated in the margins: the subcultures, red-light districts and secret nightlife of queer modern Japan. Queerness was truly perceived as separate from mainstream society only from the late nineteenth century, when the Meiji Restoration of 1868 marked the end of the medieval Edo period and the beginning of the modern era. As detailed in the historian Mark McLelland's books *Male Homosexuality in Modern Japan* (2000) and *Queer Japan from the Pacific War to the Internet Age* (2005), same-sex eroticism, sexual practices and homosociality – particularly between men – in pre-modern Japan were inextricably intertwined with mainstream society under a system known as *nanshoku* (male colours). Subsequent exposure to Western hegemonic ideas introduced the idea of distinct sexualities, as well as the first attempts to medicalize and discourage so-called homosexuality, or *dōseai*.

BELOW: A still from Toshio Matsumoto's 1969 drama *Funeral Parade of Roses*, a transgressive art film set in the water trade of the underground gay world and featuring *gei bōi* protagonists.

In the decades following the Restoration, through the rise of Japanese imperialism and the Second World War, the country's queer population was both marginalized and thriving. While Japan's nationalist, pro-natal policies stigmatized same-sex relationships, within the country's military forces homosociality and homoeroticism swelled.

The mid-1940s and 50s brought the country's first 'gay boom' with the end of Japanese militarization and the start of American occupation. Japan's largest Gay Town, Shinjuku Ni-chōme, came to serve as a queer red-light district for both Japanese and American GI clientele. The *danshō* were the first proto-drag queens to appear in this dangerous new world: female-presenting sex workers who roamed the streets at night. Most contemporary sources remember *danshō* as simply cross-dressing male prostitutes, but in interviews many articulate identities closer to what we would now consider transgender women. Regardless, the post-war *danshō* led difficult lives, often looking in from the outside at families and the heteronormative domestic joy they could never find.

Very different were the *gei bōi* and *blue bōi* who rose to popularity between the mid-1950s and the 1980s. As famously depicted in Toshio Matsumoto's film *Funeral Parade of Roses* (Bara no Sōretsu; 1969), *gei bōi* were an ostentatious new movement of androgynous and glamorous youths working the seedy nightlife ('water trade') of the cities.

Like *danshō*, *gei bōi* expressed a wide range of identities by today's standards, from effeminate men to third-gender people to transfemme women. Unlike the *danshō*, who could venture out only at night, *gei bōi* were bold and economically aspirational, and had jobs entertaining masculine gay customers (*homo*, distinguished from *gei* at that time) or singing chansons in lounges. Some of these *gei bōi* became minor celebrities in mainstream society – a particularly well-known example being the singer, actor and television personality Akihiro Miwa, who rose to fame after debuting as a *gei bōi* at the age of seventeen in 1952.

By the 1980s, as queer communities and terminology continued to evolve, *gei bōi* branched into two groups. Those who tended towards sex work and its adjacent industries became known as the pejorative *new half*, closely synonymous with the English 'she-male'. Meanwhile, *gei bōi* who gravitated towards singing, dancing and other more performance-orientated ventures gradually came to be called by (and to self-identify with) a new term from abroad: 'drag queens'.

Simone Fukayuki, based in the western Kansai region, was one of the first gender-bending performers to self-identify (somewhat reluctantly) as a drag queen. She began performing in 1982 as a chanson singer, taking her first name from a French actor and her second from a rare alternative reading of the Japanese name Miyuki – a beautiful and poetic name that, she imagined, a geisha might hold. Drawing on the rich artistic scene of Kyoto and the lively social community of Osaka, in 1989 Fukayuki partnered with the late drag queen Glorious to found the longest-running

"These Queens became the unsung heroes of Japanese Gay Towns, protecting the very brick-and-mortar establishments that constitute those spaces."

ABOVE: Longtime performer and hyper-queen, Afreeda Obreat. In a (literally) underground venue, not far from the imperial palace, *Diamonds Are Forever* has often been the subject of Japanese gender and queer studies, and considered iconic for its commitment to pageantry, old school music, and counter-cultural ethos.

OPPOSITE: Comedian and television personality Matsuko Deluxe is a great case study of 'queen character' talents popular on mainstream Japanese television. Deluxe is also notable for being openly gay (still relatively rare among celebrities in Japan today).

drag show in Japan, *Diamonds Are Forever*. Held on the last Friday of every month in Kyoto's subterranean club Metro, *Diamonds* is a drag show with ties to avant-garde art, club kid culture and HIV/AIDS activism, espousing a strong countercultural ethos in everything it does.

From the 1990s onwards, active drag circles proliferated in Japan, influenced by the classic Australian film *The Adventures of Priscilla, Queen of the Desert* (1994). Some of Japan's now iconic drag queens, such as Queen Margarette, began performing after the film sparked their interest in celebrating queer femininity in ways rarely accepted by the macho gay scene of the time. Others, among them the dancer and HIV/AIDS activist Madame Bonjour JohnJ, had already been engaging in experimental performance art, and accepted the name 'drag queen' after the fact (much as Fukayuki had, ten years earlier). This was the decade that truly cemented the reign of Japan's drag performers.

Eventually, drag queens came to fill an important niche within Gay Towns, becoming mamas and proprietors of many of the tiny gay bars wedged into a few dense city blocks. While perhaps not as visible as such American drag legends as Marsha P. Johnson and Sylvia Rivera (see pages 179–181), these queens became the unsung heroes of Japanese Gay Towns, protecting the very brick-and-mortar establishments that constitute those spaces.

THE *QUEEN KYARA*: MAKING IT BIG ON THE SMALL SCREEN

Japanese drag is still very marginalized, and the scene is narrower than those in other countries. Even in Tokyo, which arguably boasts more drag queens than any other Japanese city, very few can make a living solely as performers or even as bar hostesses. It's a far cry from the massive urban drag scenes in the United States, for example, where a showgirl can work every night of the week.

Still, some girls in Japan have found mainstream media success of which most can only dream. Among them are the so-called *queen kyara* (queen characters) who appear regularly on Japanese television. Best represented by the amazingly successful Matsuko Deluxe, these *queen kyara* are often outlandish gay or transgender comedians who appear as femme-presenting hosts, competitors and panel members on Japan's never-ending variety shows.

Another queen who has broken into the mainstream is Shinjuku Ni-chōme's own Durian Lollobrigida, who built her career as both a solo singer and a member of the drag queen girl group Happo Fubijin (All-Around Uglies) alongside Esmralda and Chiaki Whitmi. She has since become a staple of major Pride events throughout the country, appeared regularly on various late-night shows, and debuted as a mainstream actor in Daishi Matsunaga's film *Egoist* (2022).

Still, drag and queer culture in general rarely feature significantly in Japanese national broadcasting, as the conservative government continues to discourage gay and trans visibility. The best places to encounter the country's drag scene are not in the sparkling studios and on television sets, but in the tiny snack bars, underground clubs and streets of the Gay Towns.

THE NEIGHBOURHOOD GIRLS

Drag bars are still the places to see Japan's drag queens, particularly those from earlier times when drag shows were less common. Snack bars that have drag queens as their hosts can be found here and there throughout Tokyo, but the easiest to access are the Campy! bars in Ni-chōme and Shibuya Parco, established by the drag queen Bourbonne in 2013 and hosted by a crew of fellow queens during their night-time hours.

Japan's drag culture varies greatly by area – a hangover from the small islands' mountainous terrain and rigid historical feudal system, which cultivated strong regional identities – and such cities as Osaka and Nagoya have particularly significant bar-queen cultures. In Osaka, these bars, such as the popular Ludo, can be found in the Doyamacho and Shinsaibashi districts, while Nagoya's queens host, bartend and occasionally perform in Bar Piece (run by the famous Nagoya queen Lyra-h Grail) and others.

From about 2010, when *RuPaul's Drag Race* began showcasing American styles of drag to the world, a more dance- and performance-focused wave of drag emerged in Japan. Rather than dress up to serve behind a bar or chat up customers, these queens live for the stage, the lip-sync and the Mackaella dip. In Nagoya, such events centre on LOVER:z's Metro party (not to be confused with the *Diamonds* venue, Club Metro, in Kyoto) organized by American-born queen Miku Divine. In Tokyo, drag shows of this kind are easiest to find in the international sectors of Ni-chōme. The event organizers at Eagle Tokyo Blue also manage the much larger, high-production, semi-annual event Opulence, where some of the best local queens perform alongside RuGirls from overseas.

Finally, the rising influence of foreign queer media in Japan has generated interest not only in *Drag Race*, but also in American house balls through the television series *Pose* (2018–21) and *Legendary* (2020–22), and, of course, Jennie Livingston's documentary *Paris Is Burning* (1990). Drag queens occupy a unique place in the fabric of Japan's ballroom society as visibly queer participants who have helped to reconnect the formerly hetero-dominated world of Japanese ballroom with the LGBTQ+ scene beyond. *Kiki* and major balls almost always open with a showcase of local drag talent, and the runway is a great place to see them compete for Best Dressed, Drag King/Queen Makeup, Hair Affair or Designer's Delight.

"Gay Towns and drag shows are the place to find safety, inspiration and joy."

ABOVE: Nattmara, the mother of Haus von Schwarz, is one of the longest-performing foreign drag queens in Japan. As evidenced in her costumes and style, Nattmara's roots lie in the Visual Kei scene of the early 2000s and the club kid movement of the mid-2000s.

OPPOSITE: Canadian-born Sasha Zamolodchikova and Australian-born Belgium Solanas make up the the Kiss Kiss Bang Bang Art Collective, representing mixed-media avant garde drag. Solanas still lives in Japan today, and performs throughout the country.

WEIRD DRAG AND TOKYO CLUB KIDS

The story of the drag community in Japan would not be complete without exploring the fringe and alternative drag scenes. These subcultures-within-subcultures cultivate a strong sense of queerness and rejection of the status quo through their goth, horror and avant-garde aesthetics.

One of the most influential movements within 'weird drag' was the Tokyo club kid era of the mid-2000s. Led by musical artists and fashion influencers, such as DJ Sisen Murasaki, Diva Selia and Preta Porco, it coincided perfectly with the world's growing interest in Harajuku fashion subcultures, such as Lolita and Decora, edgy subversions of the 'Cool Japan' narrative that was being pushed as the national brand strategy. The Tokyo club kids were inspired by Western fringe figures such as James St James, Leigh Bowery and Boy George, and eagerly incorporated these styles with Japanese pop culture and contemporary art in their own fashion ensembles. Many of these key players are still active at such alternative events as Tokyo Decadance and Dark Castle.

In a similar vein, and often with some overlap, Tokyo's famous monthly fetish party Department H has served as a meeting place for some of the city's most eccentric and unapologetically strange inhabitants.

Typically emceed by Margarette and kicked off with a grand march of local girls, such as Durian, Bouillabaisse and the late Onan Spelmermaid, Department H is a playground for the weird and kinky, watched over by schoolmarm-like drag queens.

'There has always been a role for drag queens at Department H,' Durian told me. 'It's a place where men, women, straight people, queer people are all mixed together. Women get harassed sometimes by male attendees … If a man scolds them, there might be a fight. If a cisgender woman scolds them, they don't listen. But when a drag queen says "Hey, stop that!" somehow it works out.' With drag queens serving as de facto hostesses, security guards and ethics committee, Department H has continued successfully for more than thirty years. Drag shows, woven into the event's mix, are generally old-school Japanese style: slapstick, campy and high in ribald humour.

In recent times, Tokyo's alternative drag collective Haus von Schwarz has striven to protect these spaces and nurture weird drag of all kinds. Several of the performers, including Swedish-born Nattmara and American-born Julia Your-Makeup-Is-Terrible, are long-time residents of Japan who hail from the original Tokyo club kid movement, helping the contemporary weird drag scene to maintain its ties to older countercultural communities. It is at these alternative shows that you can watch queens pour blood over their heads, give birth to demon babies on stage, and perform human sacrifices. All play-acting, of course.

INTERNATIONAL QUEENS, JAPANESE QUEENS AND THE PEOPLE IN-BETWEEN

The queer community of Japan faces the daunting task of fighting the myth that this is a homogeneous country. Japan has always been a diverse place, home to Indigenous groups including the Ainu and Luchuan (Ryukyuan) peoples, as well as countless descendants of Korean, Chinese and Filipino immigrants. Over the last few generations, the number of foreign residents from countries all over the world has increased substantially.

The drag community further drives this point home. You will meet queens who are Japanese, Japanese American, from foreign countries, from multi-ethnic backgrounds, or whose families have lived in Japan for generations without ever gaining citizenship. Most people in Japan are navigating strange and interesting aspects and intersectionalities of their identity. While the government lags behind those of other countries in granting minorities – particularly transgender people – legal rights and protection, Gay Towns and drag shows are the place to find safety, inspiration and joy. Next time you visit, come and join us!

OPPOSITE: Brazilian-Japanese queen Labianna Joroe, who has been instrumental in building Japan's mainstream drag presence in recent years with projects such as the celebrated drag show, *Opulence.* Labianna has a presence in Japanese television and queer rights activism, as well as ballroom where she is the mother of the Japan chapter of international kiki house Pinklady.

FROM *BARANGAY* PAGEANTRY TO WORLD-CLASS STUNTS

Tsarlotte Lucifer

Drag in the Philippines is ruled by a simple philosophy: entertainment at all costs. That's an oversimplification of what are considered the hallmarks and central tenets of Filipino drag culture, but it is what really makes the scene so special and vibrant; it is about finding fun and glamour in anything, even, for that matter, in almost nothing.

ROOTS IN PAGEANTRY

To understand the rise of Filipino drag, it's necessary to look at the beauty pageant scene and how it intertwines with local drag. If you ask any queer Filipino about their first exposure to drag, most will say that they either watched or helped out at local community pageants, often called 'Miss Gay' or 'Miss *Bakla*' (*bakla* is a term used for both 'gay/queer' – anyone that doesn't fit gender norms, more commonly used for trans women). These pageants, which are modelled on such competitions as 'Miss Universe', are closely akin to drag pageantry in the United States, with swimsuit segments, evening-gown competitions and talent shows in which one sees both world-class singing and bucking across a rickety stage, done with reckless abandon and boundless confidence. This experience is part and parcel of most, if not all, home-grown Filipino drag artists. How do you think people like Marina Summers managed to survive the foreign drag scenes?

Filipino pageantry started in 1908, during the American colonial period, with the Manila Carnival Queens, who competed in the Manila Carnival. The Manila Carnival Queens' competition was held until 1938, but the title of 'Miss Philippines' was only coined in 1926, when it split from the Manila Carnival to become its own competition, but it led to the Philippines becoming a big name in the international pageant scene, winning a total of fifteen crowns in the Big 4 ('Miss Universe', 'Miss World', 'Miss International' and 'Miss Earth'). But what does pageantry – which is mostly the preserve of cisgender and heterosexual women – have to do with drag and the queer community? The answer lies in the way these events helped to kick-start local pageants dedicated to drag artists and trans women. First seen in the 1950s, these pageants (a significant one being 'Miss Gay Philippines') helped poor queer people not only to reclaim their beauty, when they were shunned from most of society and painted as 'unfit' to be considered beautiful by most, but also to earn money and recognition for themselves and their families. The pageants offered a few thousand Philippine pesos for cash prizes (1,000 Philippine pesos is equivalent to around US$20 today), and such a sum could be life-changing for the pageant queens.

Soon enough, drag started coming into the mainstream public consciousness through films and media. A key example is the film *Ang Tatay Kong Nanay* (*My Father, My Mother*; 1978), starring the Filipino comedy icon Dolphy Quizon and directed by Lino Brocka, the story of a gay beauty-salon worker raising his lover's child after the lover went to work abroad in order to support the child. It was one of the first films in the Philippines to explore the hardships of being not only a queer person, but also a drag artist. Despite the stereotyping and slightly clunky

PREVIOUS PAGE: Taylor Sheesh, the Philippines' premier Taylor Swift impersonator.

ABOVE: One of the most famous photos of Pura Villanueva, first winner of the Manila Carnival Queens' competition.

OPPOSITE: The line-up of trans women for the swimsuit section of a beauty pageant (often referred to as 'Miss Gay' pageants).

handling that arise from the film being a product of its time, it is (for 1978, at least) a surprisingly positive depiction of drag and queer parenthood.

DRAG UNDER OCCUPATION

As in many colonized countries (and for the Philippines it was a case of triple occupation: Spain, America and Japan at various times throughout its history), drag has been through a lot, ranging from criminalization to public shaming and worse. An early proponent of drag in the country, Walterina Markova (1924–2005), was subject to many such horrors. He experienced physical abuse from his older brother for his flamboyance and gender-nonconformity, which is sadly a common experience for queer kids in the Philippines. He later joined a group of stage performers who cross-dressed in clubs and bars, and that led him to perform in nightclubs, specifically exotic dancer shows and gay pageants in Angeles City, before he started performing in Pasay.

One story Markova told in an interview was of performing at a floor show for American soldiers (who were present in the Philippines even after

the US occupation ended, before the Second World War). The backstage staff told all the dancers, but not the customers, that Markova was not a cis woman, and this led to an American soldier picking him up and inviting him to perform at the Officers' Club.

When the Second World War started, Japan occupied various part of the Pacific, including the Philippines, and this ushered in a dark time for local queer people. Markova was a 'comfort gay', in a similar way to the 'comfort women' who were forced into sexual slavery by the Japanese. Comfort gays were gay men who experienced the same sexual slavery, but were treated worse because of the criminal status of homosexuality. Exposed by Japanese soldiers after they were taken to their hotel rooms, Markova and his friends were raped, tortured and forced to carry out manual labour for a month, before they escaped in the dead of night and fled to other parts of the Philippines, where they performed in cabarets. Markova recalled in interviews that he and his friends would collect trophies, cash prizes and winning bids against cis women, owing to the sheer glamour and elegance they displayed when compared to women from rural areas, who hadn't had the chance to see what the women in the cities were doing. After the war, Markova retired from the stage and from drag, and took up various jobs, including working as a make-up artist for clubs and film productions.

We know Markova's story because he survived. Sadly, he was one of the few who did; all other members of his group were killed in a raid before the Japanese occupation was lifted. But he was one of the even rarer few who had a film made about his life. His work as a make-up artist allowed him to become friends with film producers and crew, and that led to his story being picked up by the reporter Loren Legarda and made into the film *Markova: Comfort Gay*, which was released in 2000. This film also starred Dolphy, and in it three actors (Dolphy and his sons Eric Quizon and Epy Quizon) depicted Markova at various stages of his life. The 2000s were not kind to queer culture in the Philippines, and the film, again, suffers from being too strongly of its time, but it is important for shining a light on the hidden struggles of comfort gays.

THE MODERN AGE OF DRAG

Approaching better times, drag in the Philippines today is a kaleidoscope of identities, ideas, influences and inspirations that honour and innovate on the work and history of its predecessors (some of whom are still involved in the scene). The local drag scene is now strongly influenced by the local franchise of *RuPaul's Drag Race*, but still it has its own energy, and it exemplifies the idea of entertainment at all costs.

Any queer kid in the Philippines who grew up in the 2000s and 2010s can attest to having found and seen more and more queer icons on

ABOVE: Poster of *Markova: Comfort Gay*, the 2000s movie based on Walterina Markova's life, starring Dolphy.

OPPOSITE: Precious Paula Nicole performs at *RuPaul's DragCon LA* in 2023.

> "For much of the community though, young queer kids' exposure to modern drag came from going to salons."

television. One such icon is Vice Ganda, a television personality who, as a gay man, showcases gender-nonconformity and drag in a comedic yet authentic way. His catchphrase, 'Boom, panes!' (a common interjection, much like 'boots!' within the lingo of the ballroom scene), and nickname 'Unkabogable' (a term that means 'unbeatable', using the Filipino gay slang term 'kabog', which means 'to beat'), are deeply entrenched in many people's minds, and he even has his own successful make-up line.

For much of the community, though, young queer kids' exposure to modern drag came from going to salons. Many *bakla*s and trans women old and young (but especially old) work and thrive in these campy, feminine, gossip-filled spaces, and more often than not people visit to see the girls get ready to go out or to do a show, sweeping cheap make-up on to their faces and coiffing their brightly dyed hair into glamorous hairstyles.

The emphasis on 'especially older' is extremely important. The Philippines has one of the best-known queer elder collectives in the world, the Golden Gays. This group, which was founded in the 1970s by the

local politician and staunch AIDS activist Justo Justo, is a community of older gay men and drag elders who live together in a house in Pasay. Forced out of their family homes when they were young, and banding together even as they were obliged to work on the streets, many of these queer elders – affectionately called *lolas* (grandmothers) – perform in drag to generate income, since there is minimal support from the government. The Filipino concept of *bayanihan* (community) really came through for the Golden Gays as they struggled through the COVID-19 pandemic with no gigs or fundraising opportunities; online drag shows and fundraisers were held for them, and local queer community members sent them supplies. The Golden Gays are icons and bastions of the Filipino queer community, and in 2023 they featured on the second series of *Drag Race Philippines* as the makeover challenge participants, creating a tangible new wave of support for these queer elders.

PREVIOUS PAGE: Manila Luzon attends *RuPaul's DragCon LA* in 2019.

ABOVE: One of the queens from the Golden Gays group, performing at a local event.

OPPOSITE: Myx Chanel, one of the new faces of Philippine drag and the host of *Beke Nemen*, a local series of viewing parties and themed drag nights.

THE NEW GENERATION

Today's drag in the Philippines has such community icons as *Drag Race Philippines'* first winner, Precious Paula Nicole; Slaytina (host of the Crypt of Slaytina, one of very few spaces in the Philippines to focus on alternative drag); Viñas DeLuxe; Lady Gagita; and even a Taylor Swift impersonator, Taylor Sheesh, who went viral in 2023 for her Eras Tour re-creations and mall shows.

However, a more recent and arguably more important development is the rise of alternative drag and drag kings. This is still a new frontier, but since 2017, a plethora of new performers, new spaces and new forms of drag have arisen in the Philippines scene, helmed by such people as Myx Chanel, Slaytina, Inah Demons, Alpha Venti and Panthera Arma (the first hearing-impaired drag artist in the country). These trailblazing artists have shown the people of the Philippines new sides of drag in local bars and performance spaces.

Along with these developments, there are shows – such as *Drag Den*, hosted by Manila Luzon – that present a more Filipino drag, with their *dragdagulan* (wrecking-ball battle) segments inspired by local *barangay* (a term used to define a village or a ward in the Philippines, which comes from the boats that ancient Filipinos used to transport themselves to pageants) and their tendency to invent stunt competitions for their talent segments with a reckless abandon that most international viewers have never seen before. If you think Tandi Iman Dupree's ceiling split at the 'Miss Gay Black America' pageant in 2001 was wild, look at the Filipino drag girls, who won't hesitate to throw themselves through basketball hoops to land in jaw-dropping splits.

All this goes to show that the drag scene in the Philippines is thriving, and that new forms of drag entertainment are being cultivated all the time. International audiences just have to get to know them and ensure they thrive. It is exciting to speculate about where Filipino drag will go from here, especially now that the artists have the chance to showcase their talent on an international stage with televised drag competitions, and with the rise of drag kings and other forms of drag that bring refreshing things to the table.

"The drag scene in the Philippines is thriving, and new forms of drag entertainment are being cultivated all the time."

OPPOSITE: Inah Demons, digital artist, clown, and part of the Philippines' vanguard of drag kings.

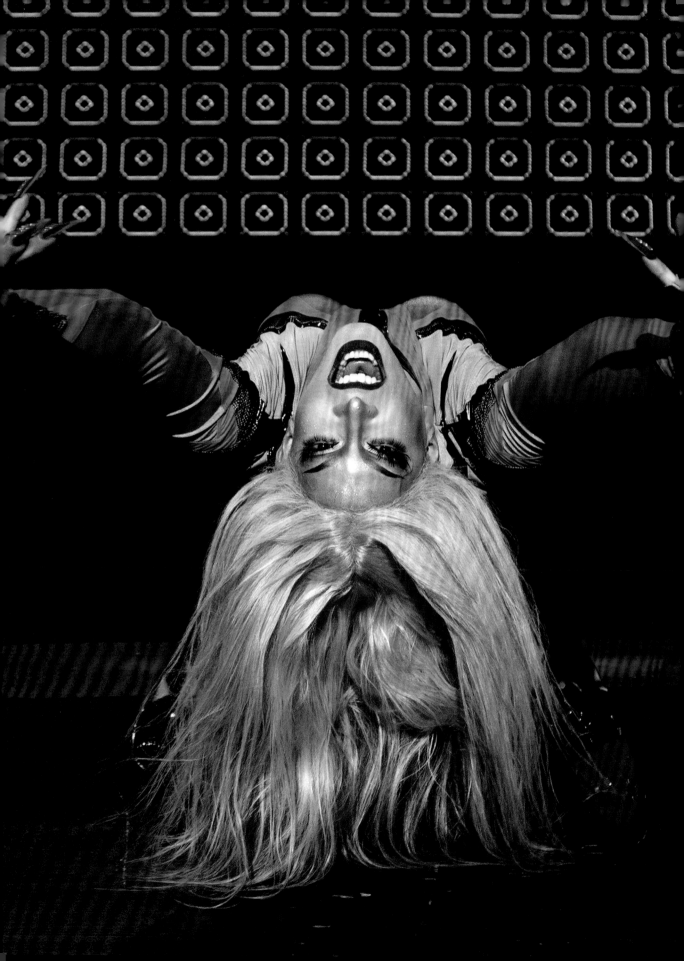

FIERCE AND JOYFUL TRANSFORMATIONS, FROM TIFFANY'S TO THE WORLD STAGE

Presley Stewart

Thailand is known for its incredible food, culture and, of course, beautiful people. However, we would all be doing ourselves a disservice if we did not also enjoy the country's beautiful and rich queer history, which goes hand in hand with its drag scene. In 1909 Thailand enacted a law that criminalized anything that might fall under the umbrella of homosexuality, from sex to queer performance. Thankfully, that law was reversed in 1956, opening the door to safer lives for queer Thai people and welcoming the dawn of queer entertainment in the country.

THE DAWN OF IT ALL

The first drag show in Thailand was created for a private birthday party, a cabaret-style show by a gorgeous crew of drag queens from the Philippines. Vichai Lertritraugsin, who was in the crowd, immediately started looking for other businesspeople with whom he could collaborate to start a cabaret bar in Pattaya, which would be the first of its kind in Thailand. In the meantime Lertritraugsin decided to host the country's first ever drag shows at his own venue, the Tulip Bar. People raved about them, and word spread so quickly that he had no choice but to work on opening a bar specifically for such shows.

Lertritraugsin eventually met Sutham Phanthusak, and together they created a drag bar in the city of Pattaya, not far from Bangkok, that could seat up to 500 people, for Thais and tourists alike. This bar, Tiffany's, is generally said to mark the real beginning of drag in Thailand in 1975. At the time, Thailand was introducing its First Economic Development Plan to boost tourism, especially in Pattaya, with the aim of improving the country's economy and status. The focus on attracting tourists meant that cabaret performances, like Tiffany's Show, grew larger and larger across and all around the country, which led to a significant piquing of interest in drag.

PREVIOUS PAGE: Pangina Heals performs during 'RuPaul's Drag Race British Invasion' in 2022.

ABOVE: The theatre of Tiffany's Show in Pattaya.

OPPOSITE: Contestants in the kathoey (ladyboy) beauty pageant.

PUBLIC RECEPTION

Thailand, for the most part, has a positive relationship with queer people and drag queens. Homosexuality is legal in the country, but in many provinces gay people can't get married, have any other kind of legal union or adopt children. A national movement to change this has been in the works for years, and is gaining popularity and support every year. For drag queens and transgender people, life looks a little different. Drag queens and those who show other forms of alternative gender expression are well regarded in theory, but it isn't always rainbows and sunshine in terms of how they are treated. Nevertheless, on websites aimed at tourists, drag is listed as a top reason to visit Thailand, and glitzy drag and cabaret bars always feature prominently in guidebooks. Drag is Thailand's pride and joy from the perspective of tourism, but also for many Thai people. Most non-queer Thai people are familiar with drag through the comedic folk band Siang Isan and the film franchise *Hor Taew Taek*; male performers or characters cross-dress in both of them.

In a study carried out in 2023, researchers from Thammasat University found that, for the most part, drag queens in Thailand don't struggle with acceptance by their families. The same could be said of relationships. Many of the queens who were interviewed said that men didn't like them because being a drag queen was too closely aligned with being feminine, or even too chubby. However, if they found a partner who respected their work, they felt confident in their drag careers and their relationships. The study found that older generations in Thailand are less familiar with drag queens, but are generally interested in learning or simply don't care much one way or the other. There is a national push in politics for better recognition of drag queens, queer people and other forms of gender-queer expression, and although it is going strong and steady, there is still work to be done.

NOTABLE STYLES, FIGURES AND MEDIA

Thailand's drag queen is fierce, beautiful and joyful, and the country's rich drag history is replete with gay men, gay women, transgender people and even straight folks. The emphasis is on the idea of transformation, so as long as there is a clear difference from who you were before the make-up – in appearance and even personality – you are doing good, artistic drag.

"The country's rich drag history is replete with gay men, gay women, transgender people and even straight folks. The emphasis is on the idea of transformation."

RIGHT: Miss Renata Ferreira from Germany in National Costume on stage in the transvestite and transgender beauty pageant, Miss International Queen, 2013, at Tiffany's Show theatre in Pattaya city.

In some parts of Thailand, drag queens are expressive, fun, silly performers who might appear as a drag queen for only a short time, and don't feel the need to emulate the look of cisgender women. *Naang* or *kathoey* shows, on the other hand, involve performers who want to pass as a woman at all times, even when they don't perform to build an illusion of womanhood. This isn't standard across the country, but it is common in some places, especially where there are more competitive cabarets. Neither is seen as better than the other, and all are valued equally highly. Thailand's drag is a mixed bag, and that is what makes the country's art style so cool.

Many countries represent their drag on television, and Thailand is no exception. One of the most notable shows is *Drag Race Thailand*, which first aired in 2018, hosted by Pangina Heals and Art Arya. Pangina has been described as one of the most recognizable and beloved drag queens in Asia. Getting her break at a Lady Gaga impersonation competition in 2010, she is notable for her waacking street-dancing style, which she learned in Los Angeles, and for House of Heals, the drag bar she owns in Bangkok. Art Arya studied fashion in Paris, and her eyes were opened to drag by the first season of *RuPaul's Drag Race* in 2009. The two hosts' love of drag shines through, and they meld their love of fashion and their experience of growing up gay in Thailand to celebrate and highlight other queer performers. Winners of the show include Natalia Pliacam, who started doing drag in 2006, when she entered and won the Thai 'Miss

ABOVE: Still from *Beautiful Boxer* (2003).

AC/DC' beauty pageant. As well as being the first winner of *Drag Race Thailand*, she is the first plus-size winner in the entire franchise. Angele Anang was the second winner of the competition in 2019. Starting out as a Beyoncé impersonator, she gained international fame as she rose through the ranks in transgender cabarets at Calypso in Bangkok.

There has even been a slew of movies dedicated to cross-dressing, gender-bending and drag performers, based on real and fictional stories. *The Iron Ladies* (2000) tells of the Thai national volleyball team of 1996, who fought their way to victory – although everyone doubted them because the team was made up of transgender women and gay men. *Beautiful Boxer* (2003), meanwhile, explores the life of a boxer who is trying to win matches to make money for drag and eventual surgery.

OUT ON THE TOWN

"Thai drag queens often pay homage to their roots in Pattaya-style drag shows, and that contributes to the family feeling of these cabarets."

All of Thailand's cities have their own distinctive nightlife with glitz, glam and drama, but wherever you go, you are always in for a show that displays the beauty of drag. There are a few variations, from competitive cabarets and Pride events to nightclub performances and even seated shows. Queens typically lip-sync, dance or sing live, and comedy sets, drag kings and more masculine performers are few and far between.
In Bangkok, you're always in for a wild ride. The district of Silom is the city's gay haven, separated into two: Soi 2 and Soi 4. Silom Soi 2 is a strip of gay bars perfect for those who like to party in vibrant clubs, like DJ Station, a three-storey club perfect for getting your groove on or for watching the drag shows that happen just before midnight. Silom Soi 4 is ideal for those who prefer a more chilled environment. At The Stranger, a gay bar, guests, dancers and even bartenders take shots in pretty masks while seated for vibrant drag shows. In both areas you'll see a blend of Thai people and tourists from all over the world. The drag shows of Bangkok are typically themed – Gaga Night, for example, or Business Realness, almost like ballroom in Los Angeles or New York – and less competitive than the cabaret-competition shows that are more popular in other parts of the country.

The neighbourhood of Patong in Phuket is known as the gay Paradise Complex. People come to enjoy saunas, cabarets, go-go shows and discos. The Boat Bar is Patong's oldest gay disco, where two drag shows are held each night. Simon Cabaret is one of Paradise Complex's oldest drag cabaret shows, and is often considered one of the best drag shows in the whole of Thailand. There's also My Way, another of Phuket's longest-standing gay bars, with an extensive list of drag shows. Sometimes, My Way even worked with ZAG, a local queer bar for women, to create shows that gay men and women could enjoy together. Anyone coming to the Paradise Complex for drag shows should expect to see many cut-throat

OPPOSITE: Performance of 'Big Spender' in the Simon Cabaret in Patong Beach.

cabaret contests. Patong's drag environment is like that of Bangkok's Soi 4, with people venturing out mainly to sit and watch, rather than a club or party environment. This scene may be small, but it's mighty fierce.

Pattaya is the beginning of Thailand's drag. Cabaret-style shows, where queens compete for crowns and cash prizes, are often the only ones you will see there. Tiffany's is the epicentre of these shows, as one of the biggest and having kicked off cabaret and drag in Pattaya and, indeed, all of Thailand. These are typically family-friendly and accessible to both queer and straight audiences, as are the annual city-wide events such as Pride. The drag queens wear sparkly outfits and big hair, and are generally more showy than those in Patong or Bangkok. Pattaya is even popular for Carnival-style cabaret, where performers wear huge, expensive outfits that rival those of the Carnival parades in Brazil. Thai drag queens often pay homage to their roots in Pattaya-style drag shows, and that contributes to the family feeling of these cabarets.

A VIBRANT WORLD OF DRAG

Thailand is one of a kind: for its gorgeous beaches, its delicious food and, of course, its drag scene. Pride festivals, cabaret shows, drag queens, *kathoey* and more all contribute to the glory of the country. From Tiffany's in Pattaya to the House of Heals in Bangkok, global drag would not be the same without Thailand's contribution.

CABARET, BURLESQUE AND EXCESS

Jeffrey Rowe

The history of drag in France is complex, nuanced and incomplete, and its evolution unique. It is a representation of LGBTQ+ history in one of Europe's most flamboyant and vibrant nations, where drag in its numerous forms remains wholly French. Inspired by the drag culture emerging in the United States around the turn of the twentieth century, early French drag performers adopted American structures of drag performance and established a subculture of their own, distinguished from its international counterparts.

Drag in France developed according to the country's rich culture of fashion houses, cabaret and burlesque, and the sociopolitical challenges of a long history. This chapter will explore the history of drag in France from the early twentieth century in Parisian cabarets, the art of cross-dressing, the challenges of the mid-century, and the revival of queer art and its gradual progress towards mainstream cultural recognition.

CROSS-DRESSING: ART, PERFORMANCE AND SOCIAL MOBILITY

Cross-dressing and the art of transformation are as old as clothing itself. Defined as the wearing of clothing associated with the opposite sex, cross-dressing is for some a form of artistic expression, for others an opportunity for theatrical performance, and for yet others a form of gender affirmation and sociopolitical mobility. A controversial act, it was not highly regarded by religious and political authorities, but despite various legal limitations, it has for centuries offered numerous opportunities of self-expression for men, women and those in between. During the Hundred Years War (1337–1453), France and England were at loggerheads over English claims on French territory. Arguably one of the most prominent figures to come out of this tumultuous period was Joan of Arc, a young woman from rural France who inspired and led French regiments to success in battle against the English. Countless records and artworks portray her wearing male armour while parading through France. The armour was intended to protect her physically in battle, but it was especially important following her imprisonment by the English. This was both her virtue and her demise, since the English authorities charged her with the blasphemy of disguising herself in male clothing. Joan is just one example of the politicization of cross-dressing. She was not simply a prophetic virgin meant to save France, but a radicalized individual undefined by gender and impassioned by the will to serve her nation. Such a radical passion may be identified in the layers with which drag artists of the twentieth century imbued their work to push past sociocultural limitations and express themselves on the world stage.

The turn of the twentieth century was a period characterized by monumental shifts in intellectual thinking, and France was among the leaders of new artistic movements that marked out the trajectory for the rest of the century. Marcel Duchamp (1887–1968), whose work is associated with Cubism, Dada and conceptual art, provoked the art world with his infamous alter ego, Rrose Sélavy. A play on words, the name sounds like *Eros, c'est la vie* (Eros, that's life). Rrose reflected Duchamp's inspiration during his time in New York City, the epicentre of new artistic movements and the powerhouse of drag culture in the United States. Motivated by artists in New York and inspired by Greek mythology,

PREVIOUS PAGE: Nicky Doll, the host of *Drag Race France* and a former contestant on the American show with RuPaul.

OPPOSITE: A famous painting by Jean-Jacques Scherrer of Joan of Arc marching through Orléans after she helped end the siege of the city in 1429. She wears a full suit of metal armour on horseback, and is cheered on by the city's inhabitants.

Duchamp's character was meant to provoke, confuse and inflame desire by pushing past traditional social conventions of gender and sparking profound thought about the way individuals perceive one another. Duchamp was not necessarily a pioneer in the drag world, but he invigorated the movement in France by giving notoriety and sway to emerging art forms in Paris and the rest of the country. His interest reflected a major shift in the way cross-dressing came to be regarded in the art world – as an expression of self.

LA BELLE ÉPOQUE

Drag culture in France is aligned closely with the emergence of cabaret, nightlife and theatrical performance during the roaring cultural movements of the early twentieth century. French drag altered the American form of

> "Drag reached hundreds of people nightly, ensuring queer visibility in an era when same-sex relationships were frowned upon."

RIGHT: A programme for the venue Madame Arthur, which opened in 1946 and transformed Paris's local drag scene.

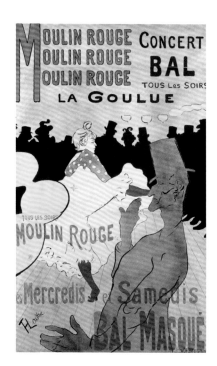

the art in intricate ways to reflect and highlight its own attitudes and culture. The vibrant queer scenes in 1920s Paris established the city as France's cultural hub, and it also became one of Europe's most visited areas for LGBTQ+ peoples (just behind London, Berlin and Amsterdam). Parisian nightlife exploded during the period of economic growth following the First World War as cabaret, jazz and theatre came together to bring life, culture and an essence of gaiety to Paris.

The first modern Parisian cabaret to open was Le Chat Noir in 1881 in the Montmartre district, and it quickly became a symbol of the city's bohemian lifestyle. Attendees were invited to small venues of this kind to dine and watch variety performances linked by a host or master of ceremonies. Cabarets – and Le Chat Noir in particular – became symbolic of the Parisian circles of intellectual freethinkers and artists, consisting of such people as Pablo Picasso, Jean Cocteau and Oscar Wilde. Rodolphe Salis, the founder of Le Chat Noir, sparked new interest in cabaret, and several new venues followed in its wake. Among them was the infamous Moulin Rouge in 1889. Artists from around Europe and the Americas flocked to Montmartre for its cabarets, circuses and other venues, to converse on politics, culture and society, making this a district where new artistic movements emerged in waves.

Many queer individuals had the opportunity to take to the cabaret stage, from the American expat Barbette to Cha-U-Kao, a lesbian 'clownesse' who motivated people to rethink the gendered profession of clowning. Barbette, a cross-dressing performer originally from Texas, awed Parisian audiences with her aerial performances at the Moulin Rouge. Her success on one of Paris's most iconic stages brought audiences from all over, including Cocteau, who ascribed her success to her contradictory appearance and 'supernatural sex of beauty'. As with Rrose Sélavy, Barbette's fame forced the audience to rethink their suppositions about gender and sexuality. These early forms of drag, while theatrical and awe-inspiring, were always radical and political beyond their intention to entertain.

As the decades of the twentieth century rolled forwards, more cabaret and performance venues opened across Paris and in other cultural centres of France. Drag reached hundreds of people nightly, ensuring queer visibility in an era when same-sex relationships were frowned on despite the nation's progressive outlook. Before Madame Arthur opened its doors in Paris in 1946, no venue had been designed to accommodate cross-dressing or transsexual performers. This truly groundbreaking venue became Paris's first female impersonator cabaret and transformed the city's local drag scene by opening a stage to queer folk. It opened during a period when legislation on male cross-dressing essentially barred men from wearing wigs, dresses or fake breasts. This forced drag performers further underground, but never entirely out of sight. Madame Arthur

ABOVE: Advertisements like Henri Toulouse-Lautrec's Moulin Rouge captured the essence of Parisian nightlife during La Belle Époque and the city's diverse forms of entertainment.

An icon of Parisian nightlife, Coccinelle was most known for her stage performances at Madame Arthur and helping to pioneer a space for trans women in Paris. Her gender reassignment was one of the most publicized in Europe following the Second World War.

became home to dozens of trans performers, from Coccinelle to Bambi, who became stalwarts of Parisian nightlife. Although neither Coccinelle nor Bambi was a drag performer as that would be defined today, they were queer nightlife performers nonetheless. They pioneered trans women's places in queer nightlife and were major proponents of the ethos that makes drag and queer culture in France unique.

Madame Arthur went through several iterations during its time in the 18th arrondissement. Its sister cabaret, Le Carrousel, was opened in 1926 as Chez Josephine by Giuseppe 'Pepito' Abatino and Josephine Baker. It was originally intended to host Baker and other Black performers during Paris's jazz era, but by 1936 it had become popular for its cross-dressing performers and its growing roster of transgender performers. The iconic facade of Madame Arthur has been maintained and its cabaret-style performances, music shows, drag performances and dance nights continue to make this area of Paris a vibrant queer hotspot with a strong history.

RIGHT: An American expat, Barbette found success on stage in Paris and became a triumphant success and staple of the city's nightlife.

THE LATE TWENTIETH CENTURY

In the late 1960s French drag underwent a rebirth. As perceptions of LGBTQ+ people gradually changed, the drag scene exploded and the nation's golden age of nightlife took Paris and other urban hubs by storm. The cultural explosion of film, fashion, theatre and cabaret transformed nightlife, especially queer nightlife, in unforeseen ways. The 1960s and 70s were a time of rapid radicalization and politization in many circles, especially that of LGBTQ+ people in France. With the establishment in 1971 of the Front homosexuel d'action révolutionnaire (Homosexual Front for Revolutionary Action), a loose Parisian movement, queer people sought to fight for their fundamental human rights in addition to forcibly creating public queer space. The movement sought to reclaim what had been lost during the Second World War, namely the legal right to cross-dress and to have queer relationships. The 1950s and 60s having brought several raids on gay bars, French queer people set out to fight for what had been taken away. An explosion of queer art resulted in a number of different mediums, of which drag was at the forefront.

Arguably one of the biggest names to come out of the 1960s and 70s was Michel Georges Alfred Catty (1931–2020), better known simply as Michou. Originally from Amiens, Michou moved to Paris in the 1950s and soon became integrated into the city's culture and nightlife. He

BELOW: Photograph of Michou in foreground surrounded by famous actors and singers and celebrity impersonators.

transformed Paris's *transformiste* culture of drag and cross-dressing. *Transformism*, or cross-dressing in English, denotes dressing in order to take on the appearance of someone else – in the case of a man, for example, the appearance of a woman – but in drag circles it meant becoming a celebrity figure. Michou opened his cabaret, Chez Michou, in 1956, and it quickly became one of the city's most popular *transformiste* venues. Guests arrived from across the country for a fine-dining and drag extravaganza in which performers transformed themselves into some of the country's most notable celebrities, such as Édith Piaf. Michou's *transformiste* style of drag and cabaret changed the way cross-dressing was used for live performances. He and his 'Michettes' became a staple of Parisian nightlife and culture in Montmartre by entertaining hundreds of curious minds and LGBTQ+ folk in safe spaces devoted to queer art. In turn, Chez Michou's inspired style of drag set the precedent for the unique qualities of French drag. The art of transformation in these venues was not necessarily to create alter egos in the way that Duchamp had or the drag artists on *RuPaul's Drag Race* do; rather, Michou's intention was to become the celebrity and bring them to small venues in the city, to adopt their mannerisms and live as a true celebrity, if just for one night.

Drag in France was by no means limited to this style, however. Drag artists across the country developed their own styles and ways of performing while staying true to their French cultural roots of cabaret, burlesque and over-the-top theatrics.

> "From theatrics to burlesque, and with their stunning fashion sense, French drag artists have carved out their own space in the history of drag."

DRAG CULTURE IN FRANCE TODAY

Following the international success of *RuPaul's Drag Race*, France's very own spin-off of the famous American show has given even more prominence to the drag movement in French culture – perhaps more than it has ever received. The French version of the show has given French drag artists the opportunity to find international success, but also, more importantly, to demonstrate their art, and to represent French drag excellence and uniqueness. From theatrics to burlesque, and with their stunning fashion sense, French drag artists have carved out their own space in the history of drag. Nicky Doll, the host of *Drag Race France* and a former contestant on the American show with RuPaul, is best known for her clothing looks, which give Parisian fashion houses a run for their money. Her style incorporates the best parts of modern French couture and she was the first to incorporate the French language and culture into their drag during her season on *RuPaul's Drag Race*. Nicky and other queens, such as Paloma, the winner of Season 1 of *Drag Race France*, set a precedent for the fashion and theatrics that are characteristic of French drag, while new arrivals on the drag scene continue to invigorate the culture with bold new ideas from all corners of France. The faces of *Drag*

Race France represent only a fraction of what the country has to offer. Local scenes in Paris, Bordeaux, Lyon and many other cities offer riveting experiences for all to encounter.

Drag shows in France today follow similar themes and nuances that are deeply entrenched in French performance styles. Theatre, fashion and the allure of cabaret are combined in a multitude of ways that continue to attract interest and maintain the unique characteristics of French drag. Drag venues hold a variety of shows, from the quintessential lip-sync style for which the art of drag is internationally renowned, to open stages, to bingo nights or after-dinner revues featuring the city's hottest artists. It is the raw talent, energy and riveting styles of drag that keep visitors returning to these venues show after show. French styles of drag are immeasurable, defined by their city, venue and drag house (like a fashion house, but where drag artists form a close 'family' to learn and grow their art), and by the vision of the drag artist themselves. French drag today consists of showgirl acts recalling the golden age of cabaret in the 1920s, transforming into well-known celebrities from Celine Dion to Piaf and Lady Gaga, and drag artists creating entirely unique personas. On a walk through Paris's popular queer districts, such as Pigalle, Le Marais or even the historic Montmartre, one is sure to come across some sort of drag venue, a gay bar or a speakeasy, where queer folk have for generations gathered to be their true selves.

OPPOSITE: Nicky Doll made her Drag Race debut on Season 12 of *RuPaul's Drag Race*. She later went on to host the French spinoff, *Drag Race France*, helping to promote French drag and queer art to the rest of the world.

BEAUTY AND JOY IN THE FACE OF HORROR AND ADVERSITY

Tsarlotte Lucifer

Despite what you might think from the portrayals in films and television, German drag is not just smoky cabaret rooms and girls with thin eyebrows and severely bobbed hair. It has a rich history of resistance, political expression and influence, and can be exemplified by the phrase 'beauty and joy in the face of horror and adversity'. From Berlin's glittery queer havens in the Weimar era, to the *Maikönigin* (May queens) of Munich, to the new wave of drag kings who hark back to pre-war styling, the drag scene in Germany is a hotbed of experimentation and progressiveness.

PREVIOUS PAGE : Barbie Q, Munich's Bolivian bombshell and the first eliminated queen of *Drag Race Germany*.

CABARET CULTURE AND THE *TUNTES*

Berlin: the capital city, the place where every Brooklyn expatriate lands and dusts off the DJ decks, the city where you can still smoke inside bars, where Central Europe never sleeps. One of the most cosmopolitan cities in Germany, Berlin can lay claim to most of the country's known drag history – and indeed queer history in general – within its concrete streets and hallowed bathroom stalls. (That may be a horrifying sentence, but it does exemplify the grit and glamour of Berliner drag.)

The important points of queer history in Berlin are well known already: the famous cabaret Eldorado, where Marlene Dietrich and Josephine Baker performed and hung out in the 1920s; the Institute for Sexual Science founded in 1919 by Dr Magnus Hirschfeld; the first known gay film, *Anders als die Andern* (*Different from the Others*), made that same year by Richard Oswald and premiered at the city's Apollo Theatre; Claire Waldoff's lesbian cabaret shows and purported queer salon; and the entirety of Nollendorfplatz (bathrooms included). But our focus here is on a queer phenomenon that cannot be found anywhere else in the world, that curious species that is unique to the drag culture of Berlin: the *Tuntes*.

The term, which can be translated best as 'sissy', refers to gay men who are wildly effeminate and – along with its English equivalent – is a slur in German gay lingo. Within drag, it refers to a subset of artists who identify as flamboyant gay men, adhere to the so-called Tuntic virtues (Shakiness, Nastiness, Shabbiness, Shamelessness, Annoyance, Cheapness, Presence, Wittiness, Elegance, and Silliness), and go through daily life in their costumes (*Fummel*). The term *Tunte* was commonly used from the mid-1950s onwards in Germany, but its current incarnation is taken from gay activists of the 1960s and 70s. A similar concept can be found in the Sisters of Perpetual Indulgence in the United States (see page 181), but *Tuntologie* is a way of life and describes a type of drag artist and activist, rather than an individual that is part of an organization, although both tend to intertwine. Both the *Tuntes* and the Sisters of Perpetual Indulgence coexist peacefully and work together in the German gay scene.

A good starting point for understanding *Tunte* culture is the work of Holger Radtke, better known as Rosa von Praunheim. Rosa is an icon of the German gay community, and his work as a filmmaker led to the formation of queer liberation groups and the beginning of the modern queer liberation movement in Germany and Switzerland. A translated quotation from his classic film *Nicht der Homosexuelle ist pervers, sondern die Situation, in der er Lebt* (*It Is Not the Homosexual Who Is Perverse, but the Society in which He Lives*; 1971) sheds some light on Tuntologie:

> *The majority of homosexual men resemble inconspicuous men who place emphasis on appearing male. The homosexual man's biggest enemy is the* Tunte. *Tuntes aren't dishonest compared to the stuffy homosexual male.*

Miss Eldorado

ABOVE: A photo of two drag queens, embodying the old school style of German drag.

OPPOSITE: Hansi Sturm, a competitor from the Miss Eldorado drag competition held in 1920s Berlin at the famed Eldorado club.

Tuntes exaggerate their flamboyant qualities and make a parody of them. In doing so, they challenge the norms of society and show what it means to be a sissy.

This quotation, and indeed the film itself, presents *Tuntes* as politically charged figures that exaggerate and 'perform' flamboyancy in order to push back against societal norms, and are often present in public as their *Tunte* selves. Most *Tuntes* came (and still come) from the working class, and to this day many face marginalization even from the regular gay scene, despite their work in advocating for queer rights. *Tuntes* were one of the leading groups in persuading the German government to recognize the AIDS crisis in Germany in the 1980s and 90s, and are still at the forefront of queer rights in the German world. If you're at a queer protest in Berlin, you will most definitely see a *Tunte* marching alongside you (but more likely in front of you).

There is a newer form of *Tunte* on the scene, and that is the *Boytunte*. Where the *Tunte* presents femininity, the *Boytunte* is masculine, but in the same flamboyant, crass way. The most famous *Boytunte* is Ryan Stecken,

who appeared on Germany's version of *American Idol* (*Deutschland sucht den Superstar*) in 2014 and 2017. Although his run was short and marred by homophobic remarks from the judges, Stecken is still going strong and performs all over Germany.

DRAG AGAINST ALL THE ODDS

Munich is the main city of conservative Catholic Bavaria, Germany's most expensive city and the newest tech capital of German-speaking Europe. Most of all, however, it's a place where the idea of even having a drag scene is still surprising. This city – its rich history of arts and culture notwithstanding – is still left behind when it comes to drag.

Let's be honest: most of the drag world knows Munich only because it was the home of Bolivian-born Barbie Q, the first eliminated queen from *Drag Race Germany*. The city's drag history is certainly slightly ragged, but Munich is today a southern bastion of drag in Germany – a fact that even Germans tend to forget.

By contrast with other cities, such as Chicago, London and even Berlin, drag was never a big part of the gay scene in Munich. The emphasis on conservative Catholic faith influenced its denizens for centuries. Most gay men in the city's history wanted to 'pass', and the gay scene can be traced largely to saunas and small bars, such as Café NiL (which is part of a guided tour that focuses on where Freddie Mercury stayed and partied while he was living in Munich), Prosecco and Jeans (now unfortunately closed). Drag artists were sadly not part of history, and most have gone unrecorded.

Munich's drag history can be divided broadly into 'old generation' and 'new generation'. There is a tangible rift between the two, to the point that a sizeable contingent from one does not attend shows of the 'opposing side'. This is reminiscent of the rivalry and the culture portrayed by *RuPaul's Drag Race*, which has influenced the local scene heavily for better or worse.

The older generation is rooted in the Western practice of travesty, which is cross-dressing on stage in order to portray a character, often playing different roles instead of a set personality. They tend to style themselves in a more camp way, as is the tradition with most theatre-derived sections of drag. Older drag artists are not afraid to sing and do comedy in drag, often all in German and influenced by historical German culture. That poses a problem for the newer crowd of drag artists and drag fans, although there is a good-sized crowd that still prefers the older style.

Most newer drag artists in Munich have been inspired either by later seasons of *Drag Race* or by the flagship season of the German franchise. In fact, the younger German audience's first exposure to drag is mostly through Drag Race, whereas older audiences may have encountered drag artists in clubs. The style of the younger generation is strongly influenced

OPPOSITE: Jazz Cortes, a drag queen based in Frankfurt.

> "The drag scene in Germany is a hotbed of experimentation and progressiveness."

ABOVE: Daphny Ryan, the winner of Christopher Stree Day Munich 2023's Pumps Race and part of the old generation of Munich drag.

OPPOSITE: Medi Ocre Legend, Munich's resident AFAB drag queen and the punk creature of Munich's new generation of drag.

by modern media and the internet. More and more young representatives are becoming stunt artists, with flips and tricks or even reveals, and most are lip-syncers, and maybe dancers as well.

A small number of Munich artists are moving away from this towards live singing, stand-up comedy, pole dancing and other strands. Monique Fatigue is a drag creature and coding icon, for example; Misstress Polonia is a club-kid type of drag artist; Medi Ocre is one of the city's first female drag queens; and Tsarlotte Lucifer (the author) is a writer. The drag host, producer and singer Pinay Colada hosts a monthly lip-sync competition, *Lovers Lipsync*, which is one of the first to be open to all types of artist.

The influence of *Drag Race* can be seen in the styles of most Munich artists, to a point that it results in some unfortunate cultural appropriation (the structured wavy wigs originally taken from hair shows, for example,

which were historically Black events; white girls with braided wigs and baby hair; and such Asian stereotypes as misused kimonos and geisha styling). This is still a major problem in the scene, and it has caused strife with other scenes that want to collaborate with drag artists. An unfortunately pervasive and persistent way of thinking is preserved in the name of tradition, such as the habit of dressing up in blackface and presenting other racist caricatures for carnival season.

Munich also has a problem with featuring drag kings and other types of drag artist that aren't the norm. These alternative artists suffer from a lack of platform and of support, since there are very few shows that foreground alternative drag. There are nevertheless a few kings of note in the city, including Ruben Tuesday, who is also the producer of most drag king-focused shows and Munich's trailblazer for kings.

Munich's scene is still evolving, and who knows what will come next. More and more shows are focusing on different types of drag, and there is increasing awareness and support of alternative drag artists in the city.

AMERICAN AND ALTERNATIVE

"Germany's drag future could be conjectured as a world of glitter, rock stars and diversity."

Germany's drag future could be conjectured as a world of glitter, rock stars and diversity – whether racial, sexual, stylistic or otherwise. Scenes are combining and evolving at a great rate, and some are even birthing spaces and stages for drag that go beyond clubs. To look at the evolution of these new scenes, let's turn to some of the other cities.

Frankfurt is an interesting city for drag. A heavy American influence through army bases and flight connections to other parts of Europe means that the scene is more Americanized than most in the country, but it is still uniquely German. The city hosts several drag competitions, such as 'Jawbreaker' and 'Drag Slam', and most operate in the same way as American contests, with 'Jawbreaker' coming the closest to American lip-sync competitions. Drag shows are also extremely common in Frankfurt, thanks to the presence of Germany's largest Sephora, a shop supplying make-up and other essentials.

On the subject of American-style drag, the region of Nordrhein-Westphalia contains such major drag cities as Düsseldorf, Cologne and Dortmund, all – being about an hour away from each other by train – fairly interchangeable in terms of artists and shows.

The region hosts one of very few drag pageants in Germany. 'Drag Star NRW', hosted by Effi Biest, is an annual competition along American lines. The competition itself requires a pageant package (a cohesive collection of looks according to different categories, often following a central theme), involves a jury panel of several judges that give critiques, and a small interview session not unlike the question and answer portions of American beauty pageants, although it carries less pomp than, say,

OPPOSITE: LéLé Cocoon, the resident wacky glam drag queen of Frankfurt (and competitor on *Drag Race Germany* season 1).

'Miss Continental'. Nordrhein-Westphalia also offers some of Germany's first ever alternative drag shows, mainly in Cologne and Düsseldorf. One of the earliest was *Velvet Curtains*, hosted by local drag artists Merrie Genesis and Aura; it later became *VC* (with Merrie and Ophelia Amok) and *Too Much* (with Aura). These shows continue to this day, and are a good stop for anyone seeking to experience modern German drag.

ABOVE: Dean DeVille and Tracey Valentino (left and right respectively), Munich's glamour duo and bridges to the old and new generations, at Oktoberfest 2022. Prost!

OPPOSITE: Drag Star Nordrein-Westphalia 2024 poster, featuring the host, Effi Biest (centre), and the competitors (L-R, anti-clockwise: Aura, Roxy Love, Remo Rivers, Larry Long, and Menorah Tea).

THE FUTURE OF GERMAN DRAG

There is more to experience in the German drag scene. We haven't even mentioned that Berlin offers one of the first all-Asian drag shows in Germany, *Slaysians* (hosted by Vivienne P. Lovecraft), or that Düsseldorf's legendary punk club Ratinger Hof held its first ever drag show in 2022.

But now that we have presented a run-through of Germany's drag scenes and histories, you might ask, 'What's next?' The answer is: anything! There is a wider awareness of and demand for drag in Germany now, and more artists than ever are coming to the forefront and presenting their own forms of drag. Now is the best time for drag artists to make their mark on German drag history. Despite many problems, the drag scene in this culturally intriguing country is as vibrant and alive as ever.

HIGH HEELS, HIGH CULTURE

Sara Altea Balestra

Despite the long and well-known history of the *bel paese*, Italy wasn't a unified country until fairly recently, and indeed Italian started being spoken by the majority of the population only after the advent of radio and television. So, with its different accents, dialects and customs, the Italian drag scene perfectly reflects the blend of regional traditions that have flourished independently in Italy over the centuries. Italian art and queer art are inextricably linked with the country's unique history and culture, and this is reflected in the participants' choice of clothing, performance and music.

From its camp theatre origins to today's television personalities, and from Milan to Naples to every small town, drag has evolved alongside the cities, giving each area a distinctive drag style.

THEATRICAL CAMP

In general, the origins of Italian drag can be connected to theatre, since in Italy traditional theatre has often involved men dressing up as women. Until 1798, in Papal States, women were not allowed to perform on the stage, and after that date dressing up as women became a recurring gag for comedy shows and performers. This is exemplified by the many regional theatre shows in which humour is defined by stereotype and exaggeration. I Legnanesi, a comedy troupe that portrays a northern Italian family speaking in strong local accents, contains many examples of femininity being not celebrated by actors, but made fun of. In that way, the male audience does not feel threatened and can instead laugh about a depiction of womanhood that is often vernacular and simplistic. The audience members are not *surprised* by seeing a man dressed up as a woman, but they are surprised by anyone who takes that seriously.

There have been a few examples of this *en travesti* (literally 'in disguise') theatre moving to television. The trio Le Sorelle Bandiera (the Flag Sisters) – consisting of the Italian Mauro Bronchi, Tito LeDuc from Mexico, and the Australian Neil Hansen – were hired by the showman and talent scout Renzo Arbore to appear on his show on national television in 1978, after he saw them performing in a gay bar. They were initially engaged simply to sing the opening and closing jingles, but they brought the show great popularity and started releasing music and touring the country soon afterwards. In a time when the sociopolitical climate in Italy was very tense and uncertain, people turned to entertainment for distraction, and the trio's popularity grew even further. That led to their first feature films, although not without opposition from from the Catholic Church. For example, Arbore cast them in the movie *Il pap'occhio* (*In the Pope's Eye*; 1980), which he directed, with Roberto Benigni and Isabella Rossellini playing the leads. A satire against the Church, it was heavily attacked by the Catholic press. Three weeks after its release it was banned on the orders of prosecutor Donato Massimo Bartolomei 'for insulting the Catholic religion and the person of the Holy Pope'. Today these performers would probably be called drag queens, but they never used that title themselves. Even in a recent interview, Hansen said they weren't drag queens, but dancers and actors playing a role on stage.

The actor and, this time, self-proclaimed drag queen Platinette got her start in theatre in similar fashion. In 1977 a group of friends started the 'K.T.T.M.C.C.' (Kollettivo Teatrale Trousse Merletti Cappuccini e Cappelliere, which can be translated as the Theatre Kollective of Make-up Bags, Lace, Cappuccinos and Hat Boxes) and immediately started

PREVIOUS PAGE: La Diamond, winner of the second season of *Drag Race Italia* in 2022.

OPPOSITE: Le Sorelle Bandiera posing with Renzo Arbore dressed as a waiter for a sketch in 1978.

> "To foreigners, Italy already has an intrinsic camp quality, owing to such cultural quirks as dramatic hand gestures, and this renders the country's drag even more extravagant and unique."

performing *en travesti*. Their shows made fun of strict societal customs and traditions through campy, cynical humour. Platinette joined the group in 1979, at the same time as it changed its name to Pumitrozzole, and they performed together until 1986. After that, she started working more in radio, and soon afterwards was given a segment in a television news programme, to critique pop culture and society. She was noticed by the television host and journalist Maurizio Costanzo, who gave her a permanent guest spot on his eponymous show, Italy's longest-running chat show. During this time, she had the chance to talk to various politicians and other important personalities. She often shared – and to this day shares – the opinions of the political right, opposing the legalization of gay marriage and same-sex adoption, and labour protection, but that was probably the only way a drag queen could be invited to discuss politics and policy on television in a country where right-wing populism was growing fast under the government (and media channels) of Silvio Berlusconi.

In the 1970s, even singers who performed in what we would now call drag, such as Renato Zero, maintained a very conservative attitude in order to appeal to the straight crowds. Some even supported the Catholic Church in its disapproving stance on homosexuality and LGBTQ+ rights, all while singing about sex between men and wearing feminine clothing.

GOING CLUBBING

Today, drag is not seen in theatres very often, unless it is in the occasional transfer to Italy of Broadway and West End shows that feature characters in drag. There are some exceptions, however, among them the theatre group Nina's Drag Queens, which regularly performs classic pieces and new shows in drag all over the country, and Kollettivo Drag King, a theatre collective of drag kings established in 2011.

In the beginning, the influence of theatre on Italian drag made it more about attitude than about look. Drag artists would emphasize mannerisms and social behaviour, putting more effort into acting out the character than into aesthetic considerations. To foreigners, Italy already has an intrinsic camp quality, owing to such cultural quirks as dramatic hand gestures, and this renders the country's drag even more extravagant and unique. It was only in the 1990s, when drag moved primarily to nightclubs and bars and movies released about drag first broke into the mainstream, that drag performers started focusing on their make-up and what they wore. Such influential drag films as *The Adventures of Priscilla, Queen of the Desert* (1994) moved Italian drag artists to create varied characters, rather than simply doing celebrity impersonations.

Throughout the 1990s, the various cities started to develop their own specific drag identities. While drag in Rome has stayed close to its original camp aesthetic, which stemmed from theatre, the Milan scene has been influenced more by the city's fast-rising status as the fashion capital of the world. Milan's drag is therefore orientated towards club performances and minimalist fashion, but it also has a strong alternative scene for those who don't feel represented by high fashion and supermodels. An example of that alternative scene is Toilet Club, an inclusive underground party with no dress code and a drag show that features queens, kings, creatures and burlesque performers. There are no rules about genre or performance type, and there is an open stage to kick off the night, as well as two rooms with different genres of music. The Toilet community of organizers and attendees goes beyond the main Friday night party to include other events in the area and work in activism and education.

By contrast, the drag scene in Naples is influenced primarily by folklore. For example, there is a centuries-old tradition in the city called *tombole scostumate* (dissolute bingo). It was originally hosted by *femminielli*. *Femminielli* are very hard to define today, since the term has

no direct correspondence outside the Neapolitan dialect. It refers to people who present as feminine but live their identity in different ways. That includes men dressing up as women, trans women, and also people embodying a third gender. They are accepted in the social landscape of the city, and even considered to bring good luck during the games of *tombola*, which were an important part of the underground scene of the city, especially after gambling was nationalised in 1734 and subsequently banned over Christmas, as it was considered immoral and anti-Christian. Classical *tombola* games are still played at home every Christmas all over the country. Nowadays, as the figure of the *femminiello* is slowly disappearing, the *tombole scostumate* are often hosted by drag queens, who have become more of a tourist attraction than a staple of the city's tradition. The wider drag scene in Naples is vibrant and creative, and an important part of the city's social life.

In Rome, the biggest drag night is Muccassassina, which started in 1991 as a fundraiser for the activist organization Circolo di Cultura Omosessuale Mario Mieli, and is now the country's longest-running LGBTQ+ party. The name of the night, which when translated literally means 'killer cow', comes from the fact that it first happened in a former slaughterhouse, and the killer cow was supposed to be the one to avenge all her slaughtered sisters.

The party's DJs produced a parody song about far-right politician Giorgia Meloni before she became the Italian prime minister in October 2022. The song criticized a speech she gave about LGBTQ+ rights and Christian morality. It gained attention throughout the country, and was so often associated with her that she quoted it in the title of her autobiography, *Io sono Giorgia*, in 2021.

The Circolo and Muccassassina have been home to many prominent figures who have fought for LGBTQ+ rights in Italy. These include Vladimir Luxuria, who was the first trans person to be elected to parliament in Europe, after almost ten years as the artistic director of the Circolo party.

Another very important figure who worked at the Circolo is La Karl Du Pigné. La Karl was in the political secretariat of the organization, in its press office during the day and at Muccassassina every Friday night. She was a lynchpin of Italian activism, opening the Rome Pride Parade every year since the first iteration, in 1994. The Roman locals still call her 'Zia Karl', Auntie Karl, in a reverential yet affectionate way.

Zia Karl's epithet reflects the way drag families work in Italy. There are, as there are elsewhere, drag mothers and drag children, but it is much more common to have big sisterhoods, often based on the clubs or bars at which the artists perform. Since there are not many professionals – designers, wig stylists or seamstresses – working with the drag community in Italy, these 'family' members help one another out, sharing their talents and skills and getting help in return.

Southern Italy relies a great deal on such drag families or collectives. An example is Le Portinaie (the doorwomen) in Calabria. The name refers to the nosy women who were traditionally closely involved in the goings-on in their villages. This is how the drag scene can look in rural southern Italy: there might not be a long tradition of big productions, but the drag queens become part of each town's social life. There are few, if any, LGBTQ+ spaces or clubs, so drag becomes a more mundane affair. Shows may happen in the local pizzeria, in the town square or in tourist resorts, with many families in attendance. Just by performing there, they are introducing people to something the locals might never have seen before in person, creating a positive experience and real awareness of what drag is. One of the Portinaie, Lady Godiva, had her own viral moment in 2019,

when the international press picked up a story from an interview with the anti-Mafia prosecutor Nicola Gratteri. The article discussed how the local Mafia dropped its ban on homosexuality, because the son of one of its bosses was performing in drag. Godiva had previously shared her unique story on television in 2015.

HALF HUMAN, HALF RAFFAELLA CARRÀ

The inspiration behind Italian drag queens, not unlike the rest of the world, has always been the strong women who made pop-cultural history. Queer people and drag performers can relate to artists who rebelled against societal norms or forged their own paths: such icons as Mina and Raffaella Carrà.

The drag queens known as Karma B are probably the most prominent representation of drag on Italian television today. After twenty years of

PREVIOUS PAGE: Drag duo Karma B are probably the most famous contemporary drag queens in Italy, as their appearances are not limited to programmes or shows made to appeal to the more niche audience that wants to see drag, but cater to everyone watching TV or going to the theatre.

ABOVE: Mina and Raffaella Carrà during their TV variety show *Milleluci*, 1974.

cabaret and club performances, the Sicilian duo, based in Rome, embarked on national tours, then landed on television. They first appeared as judges on talent shows or guests on various networks, and now they are pundits on *Ciao Maschio*, an interview show about the evolution of masculinity. They have often talked about how their drag was inspired by Raffaella Carrà, so much so that they refer to themselves as 'Half human, half Raffaella Carrà'.

Carrà – a singer, dancer and television host – is said to have been the 'pop star who taught Europe the joy of sex', at a time when Catholic morals were prevalent. She was the first woman to show her navel on Italian television, while singing about the pleasures of sex from a woman's point of view. Her music became synonymous with fun, inspiring everyone – young and old – to sing and dance along to groovy beats about topics that were considered taboo. And, as if music and attitude weren't enough to get queer people on her side, she also supported gay rights openly at a time when 'gay' wasn't even in the Italian vocabulary. Carrà was awarded the World Pride Award in Madrid in 2017. Her iconic blonde bob made it easy for drag impersonators to portray her, being immediately recognizable and paying homage to one of the fiercest allies the Italian LGBTQ+ community has ever had.

Another immediately recognizable look for the drag and queer community was the best-selling singer Mina's iconic make-up, with her downturned smokey eye and bare face. Mina is a woman whose personal life was made very public. Her relationships created scandals that resulted in her being banned from state-funded television and radio in 1963, but the public was so enamoured with her character that there was a petition to have her back, and a willingness to turn a blind eye to behaviour that the Church and high society considered immoral. She decided to stop performing in public in 1978, and this absence from view contributed to creating the aura of an unreachable diva. This inspired drag performers to channel the character of this beloved national icon, a woman who was able to make her own choices. Queer people also recognized and shared her struggles with autonomy and liberation in a conservative country that wasn't showing any intention of changing.

CIAO BELLA!

From theatres, clubs and *pizzerie* to mainstream media, the Italian community has accomplished a great deal in a very short time and with (until recently) limited resources. Drag performers have always been hired as entertainment and to look good at parties, but now the public is interested in their opinions and experiences as queer people, and seeing them on national television. Inevitably, with more representation comes more uniformity, but the scene and its local identities and traditions remains very strong.

"Queer people also recognized and shared [Mina's] struggles with autonomy and liberation in a conservative country that wasn't showing any intention of changing."

THEATRE, SEXUAL REVOLUTION AND A NEW DUTCH WAY

Gigi Rajkumar Guerandi

For all its progressive honours and trailblazing history as a pioneer country of queer liberation, Holland – or, more correctly in this case, the Netherlands – has a drag history that is rarely formally documented. When I set out to squeeze the history of Dutch drag into this chapter, I expected to face a Herculean task, given the wealth of information there must surely be on this art form in the first country to legalize same-sex marriage. In fact, quite the opposite was true. But what does emerge is a rich tapestry of Dutch drag performance, dating back hundreds of years, that has endlessly mutated with cultural shifts over time to form a diverse national queer art form.

SHOWGIRLS AT THE SCHOUWBERG: AN UNTOLD HISTORY OF DRAG THEATRE

While the British are famous for having put men in drag during the heyday of Shakespearean theatre, when women were not allowed to perform on the stage, it is less well known that the Dutch followed suit shortly afterwards. On the boards of the Amsterdamse Schouwberg (Amsterdam Theatre) it was common for men to take female roles in plays, for a similar reason. This theatre, the first in Dutch history, was erected in 1638 and home to countless *vrouwvertoners* (woman-players) from its very first production. These actors prepared for their roles in the classic drag way: they wore full faces of make-up, donned extravagant wigs, dressed in flagrantly feminine finery and even wore 'artificial aids' – I'm imagining pillows as primitive shapewear. One documented 'woman-player', Jurriaen Baet, received a rave review from a playwright of the time: 'No man plays a father so well as Jeuriaen *[sic]* Baet plays an old woman.'

Some of these actors made decades-spanning careers out of cross-dressing, as it would have been understood then, performing female roles from as young as eighteen years old until they were well into their fifties. For instance, Abram Hendrix (sometimes known as Abraham Blank) played three times more female roles than male throughout their time at the Schouwberg. By the late 1650s, half of the theatre's male cast were playing female roles regularly. Of course, much of this theatrical drag was probably played for laughs, but still, while these performers may not have known it at the time, what they did through their art sowed the seeds for Dutch drag as we know it today. Theatrical drag artists playing up the showgirl persona are still staples of the scene and can be found at such landmark queer spaces as Lellebel in Amsterdam, unknowingly continuing a centuries-old Dutch legacy.

REVOLUTION: SEX AND DRAG IN THE LAND OF 'ACT NORMAL'

To say that the 1960s changed the trajectory of queer life – and by extension drag – in the Netherlands would be an understatement. If there is one defining element of Dutch society, broadly speaking, it is that people prioritize being ordinary, as indicated by a famous saying that goes something like this: 'Act normal, that's already crazy enough.' So, when a large-scale sexual and queer emancipation movement arrived on Amsterdam's doorstep in the 1960s, it challenged the very social fabric of the country. Seemingly overnight, the capital became the city of sex, drugs and rock 'n' roll. The seeds for an explosive cultural shift had been sown in the 1950s, with an underground queer sexual scene taking root in the harbours of Amsterdam and attracting such queer icons as the famed gay

PREVIOUS PAGE: Lady Galore is a hallmark of the Dutch drag scene and author of the 2021 autobiographical drag guide *Glitter Maakt Alles Beter* (*Glitter Makes Everything Better*).

OPPOSITE: The fleeting but potent *Provo* radical youth movement was operational from 1965 to 1967, and wholly encouraged the Sexual Revolution in Amsterdam. As one of their members said at the time, the group was all for 'complete amoral promiscuity'.

French writer Jean Genet. At the same time, a queer male youth culture was growing called *Nozems*, 'troublemakers'. *Nozems* were split into two factions: the *Dijkers* and the *Pleiners*. While the former opted for the machismo of James Dean-style Americana, clad in denim and leather, the latter adopted French chanson style and fostered feminine aesthetics and identities. Both informed drag styles to come.

Nozems were replaced in the mid-1960s by *Provo* (Provocateurs), a politicized youth group that took inspiration from the public activism of Robert Jasper Grootveld, who used exhibitionist trans people and drag performers in his own displays as well as his public orgy of 1962. During this time of change, such organizations as the NVSH (Dutch Society for Sexual Reform) and the Cultuur en Ontspannings Centrum (the Culture and Recreation Centre; abbreviated, rather aptly, to COC) pushed for transgressive gender identities and the eradication of gender binaries – radical concepts even today. Amid this rhetoric and the rising popularity of androgyny in hippie culture, drag found a cultural foothold at a time when male cross-dressing was forbidden by the authorities. The number of queer bars doubled in Amsterdam in the 1960s, platforming drag performers and bringing in droves of queer tourists, much to the dismay of the local government.

With this queer upsurge came the publication of sex journals and queer magazines, and few defined the Sexual Revolution more than *Suck: The First European Sexpaper*, the final issue of which was published in the mid-1970s and showcased 'The Virgin Sperm Dancer: An Ecstatic Journey of a Boy Transformed into a Girl for One Day Only, and her Erotic Adventures in Amsterdam, Magic Centrum'. The cover of this issue features a drag-ified form that brilliantly toes the line between Andy Warhol screen-prints and Dr Frank-N-Furter of *Rocky Horror Picture Show* fame, capturing the diamond in the rough that was this early drag.

Throughout the 1970s and 80s the country's capital developed an entire queer economy, in large part because of its new-found reputation as a queer capital of Europe. For better or worse, drag performers were busier than ever because they had never been more profitable, and kings and queens worked lavish discos and parties that catered for myriad audiences from fetish subcultures to cabaret fans. This epoch confirmed that sex would forever be important for Dutch drag; this is not to say that all Dutch drag is erotic, but rather that it is uniquely open and subversive. More than that, the very geography of queer space in the Netherlands was mapped out and constructed during the Sexual Revolution of the 1960s and 70s, and drag can still be found in these same places many decades later. The trademark queer streets and canals of Reguliersdwarsstraat, Singel, Leidseplein and Zeedijk were forged in the fires of this revolution, and popular drag locales, such as the down-to-earth pub the Queen's Head, the Parisian-inspired Bar Rouge and the dinner-theatre extravaganza that is 't Sluisje Dragshow Restaurant, are institutional remains of that renaissance. Such quintessential queens as Diva Mayday, Dolly Bellefleur and Miss Windy Mills have stomped down the avenues and graced the stages of establishments that are indebted to the 1960s Sexual Revolution.

'TRAVESTIES' ON SCREEN: A HARBINGER OF DRAG RACE

One linguistic element of Dutch drag that must be understood is that for much of its history – and, arguably, until *RuPaul's Drag Race Holland* premiered in 2020 – the term for a drag performer was *travestie*, a word that translates to the obsolete term 'transvestite' and sounds like 'travesty'. This unfortunate misnomer was used to encapsulate wholly different groups, including transgender people, cross-dressers, drag artists and gender-nonconformers of all types. This helps to explain not only why Dutch drag is so difficult to pin down, but also how the country's social attachment to binary gender has informed a national style of drag that reacts directly by expanding and entirely blowing up gender performance. Think the exaggerated solid black eyeliner of a queen like Lady Galore, founder of the community-building bar competition Lady Galore's Drag Night in the 2010s, who got her start at Lellebel and whose style of

ABOVE: The cover of the final issue of *Suck: The First European Sexpaper.*

OPPOSITE: The Stiletto Sprint is a highlight event of the annual Drag Olympics held during Amsterdam Pride. Contestants comprised of queens, kings and gender-benders all race to the finish line in heels at this drag sporting hybrid.

> "It's nothing short of a miracle that *De Travestie Show* happened, more than a decade before the dawn of the Drag Race franchise."

make-up shocked when first seen in the 2000s but can now be seen all over the Dutch drag scene.

Exaggerated femininity and hyperbolic gender performance were all the rage by the turn of the twenty-first century, and no Dutch cultural artefact laid the groundwork for this better than the unlikely hit reality television programme *De Travestie Show*. Premiering in 1995 and enjoying a short but memorable run until 1997, this televised drag competition was more than a flash in the pan. Queens competed in a variety of categories in a pageant format in the style of 'Miss United States', ranging from runways to lip-syncs for a live audience of the public, drag royalty and a panel of judges led by the Dutch drag superstar Nickie Nicole. What is striking about the show – apart from the fact that it made it on to the air at all – is how much emphasis popular drag of the time placed on 'female impersonation'. These queens were truly trying to embody the feline walk of Naomi Campbell and the devastating emotiveness of Whitney Houston, in lieu of the camp and garish. It is unquestionably old-school drag to present-day eyes, but it's nothing short of a miracle that it happened, more than a decade before the dawn of the Drag Race franchise and in the wake of the AIDS epidemic that had gripped the Dutch queer community for the preceding decade.

Such bars as Lellebel, which was founded by one half of the Dutch drag duo Josephine and Daphne in the same year as *De Travestie Show* bowed out, highlight the importance of the trans community in fostering drag culture during this period. Under the official title De Lellebel, this café-turned-'multicultural transgender bar' was dolled up in the aesthetic excesses of the Baroque age – coincidentally the era in which drag found its formal start in the Netherlands – and, in a further happy coincidence, was inaugurated by Nickie Nicole. If the term *travestie* teaches us anything, it is that the various communities collected under this umbrella term all had a hand in the development of Dutch drag, and this has scarcely ever been truer than it is today. And fear not: *Drag Race Holland* is not the only Dutch drag programme since *De Travestie Show* to satiate the need for drag on-screen. *Make Up Your Mind*, a competition in which Dutch celebrities dress in drag and are judged by seasoned drag artists, began in 2021 and at the time of writing has run for four seasons.

KINGS, CLUB KIDS AND THE NEO-GENDER DRAG-TIVISM OF TOMORROW

In the present day, in line with its own history, the Dutch drag scene is at the forefront of pushing this art form into a new and exciting future. In 2020 Envy Peru, a Dutch queen of Peruvian origin who personifies the multicultural future of drag, was crowned the winner of the first season of *Drag Race Holland*. The earlier female-impersonation style of drag now

OPPOSITE: Envy Peru was the winner of season 1 of *Drag Race Holland* and, at time of writing, the only Peruvian contestant in the entire Drag Race franchise. She moved from Peru to the Netherlands at age four.

> "It is on the Dutch scene that gender-inclusive and gender-deconstructivist drag takes flight."

ABOVE: Drag performer Lady Galore embraces the drag-tivism that comes with Dutch drag, having started multiple events such as the Right To Feel Safe protest and Drag Queens United event.

OPPOSITE: Milkshake is a Dutch dance festival founded in 2012 which uses performance – most notably drag – to promote the mantra 'everything is possible'.

coexists with a burgeoning Dutch club-kid scene that reflects evolving contemporary conceptions of gender and its limitlessness. Club kids such as Taka Taka, who frequent the popular sex-positive cruising bar Club Church in Amsterdam, started drag-king workshops in this space that in 2019 gave rise to the Netherlands' first drag-king house, House of Løstbois. This gender-nonconforming drag house is one of many hallmarks of a small but determined drag reformation in the Netherlands, cementing the idea that drag is for and by anyone, regardless of assigned sex or perceived gender. On a larger scale, the drag festival extraordinaire Milkshake – whose mission statement is replete with aims of unfettered inclusivity and diversity – is an international showcase of the weird and wonderful drag the country has to offer.

Drag kings and nonconforming drag performers are by and large still at the margins of the world's drag industry, and this is certainly true in the

Netherlands too, but it is on the Dutch scene that gender-inclusive and gender-deconstructivist drag takes flight. If we look at the work of the drag king and co-founder of the House of Løstbois LatinX Charm, we observe a transgender man who uses the same theatricality, sexual playfulness, gender absurdity and technical skill as any Dutch drag artist through the ages to put his own spin on a craft that has welcomed him only in recent years. Performers of colour remain somewhat sidelined in a white-dominated country, despite an increasingly diverse and multi-ethnic population. However, these performers find solidarity and community particularly in Rotterdam, the Netherlands' other queer hub. What this generation of gender-bending drag performers lack in the catty, acerbic bite of traditional queens, they make up for in their 'drag-tivism', and the fire of social change that galvanized revolutions before is certainly present in the new-age Dutch drag of today.

Løstbois' sister house, the House of Hopelezz, is a prime example of this drag-tivism. Its chatelaine is Jennifer Hopelezz, a thick-bearded queen with wide-set hips, who founded the collective and is mother to more than fifty drag children. The House of Hopelezz's eclectic drag performers embody countless styles, from freaky club kids to sexually charged

burlesque, and Miss Hopelezz herself weaponizes her drag for entertainment and social activism in equal measure. Having co-founded the Drag Olympics and Superball – climactic events of the Dutch drag calendar – she has also been an ambassador for Amsterdam Pride and is chairperson of PrEPnu, a volunteer group fighting for access to PrEP (a drug which prevents HIV infection) in the Netherlands. And, in a series of delightful connections, she is also the co-owner of the beloved drag melting pot Club Church. But make no mistake, drag-tivism is not an age-specific enterprise, as is evidenced by the ever-energetic Victoria False, a queen and activist so old she's known affectionately as Amsterdam's 'grandmother of the drag queens'. Ultimately, drag is intrinsically political, but it has never been more political in the Netherlands than it is today.

In a country where normative normalcy and blending in are the goal, despite an unsteady but widespread tolerance, Dutch drag is screeching through the nation's sleepy towns and leaving them in the glittering dust of a tradition that's here to stay.

RIGHT AND OPPOSITE: Jennifer Hopelezz, mother of the extensive House of Hopelezz drag dynasty, is chairperson of PrEPnu, a group advocating for universal access to PrEP – a medicine which prevents the transmission of HIV by 99%.

DRAG QUEENS ON THE VERGE OF A NERVOUS BREAKDOWN!

Javier Izquierdo Cubas

The history of drag in Spain starts in the twentieth century, a period that revolved around autarchy, fervent Catholicism and the very late modernization of the state. If we are to understand the shifts of Spanish drag culture, we must juxtapose it with historical events, because while the world revolves, there's always a queer artist, somewhere, doing their thing. Location is another crucial part of understanding drag in Spain.

Discussions of Spanish culture tend to lean towards Andalusian folklore, but in fact each region possesses great cultural treasure, and the manners and lifestyle of artists differ from north to south, and from the islands to small towns to cities.

The testimony of local queens is that drag has evolved in a small number of centres. First, Madrid and Barcelona, two cities that are the main destination of the queer public. Their nightclubs, Saturday parties and festivals host the biggest menagerie of queens, both veterans and newbies. Valencia has a characteristic alternative charm, its drag artists inspired by a sexier, darker drag; we see huge platform shoes, nudity and titanic dance numbers in the Canary Islands, especially in February; and finally, Torremolinos hosts the filthiest humour. Nowadays smaller cities, such as Bilbao, Alicante and Seville, are experiencing a good deal of development in their scenes.

"These numbers involved singing coplas and cuplés, genres of popular music across Spain that often talked about marginalized characters."

PREVIOUS PAGE: Chile Güero (left) and Nativa Reina Amexicana (right) at the Cine Doré in Madrid in October 2023.

RIGHT: A *copla* by Edmond de Bries: Long live to champagne! I want to laugh, a drink to take / And now, my youth just fades / So give me some cocaine.

THE TWENTIETH CENTURY: FRENETIC WARDROBE CHANGES, FEMALE IMPERSONATORS AND CENSORSHIP

Drag arrived in Spain in 1897 with an Italian soldier called Leopoldo Fregoli, who toured Europe with his theatrical number 'Camaleonte' (Chameleon). Fregoli could change his appearance up to a hundred times in the same number, pretending to be anything from a firefighter to a young lady.

Other performers and impersonators joined the cross-dressing and gender-fluid party, among them Monsieur R. Bertin and Ernesto Foliers, and these performers were called *transformistas* ('men who would transform into somebody else', or, directly speaking: female impersonators). These numbers involved not just changing their clothes, but also singing Andalusian *coplas* and *cuplés*, genres of popular music across Spain that often talked about marginalized characters and that required a good dose of vibrato. And – since neither Madonna nor Cher was born yet – these queens impersonated Raquel Meller or Pepita Ramos at *café-concerts*.

It was the drag performer Edmond de Bries who caused a real commotion, however. A tailor from the southeastern city of Cartagena who had worked for the biggest theatre stars in the 1920s, he moved to Madrid and started putting on his own dresses. His cross-dressing numbers became a huge success. His songs mirrored the night culture, and women and gay university students especially were attracted to his shows, partly because of his exquisitely tailored dresses. He was frequently heckled or had his shows cancelled, and despite earning up to 1,000 pesetas per show (the average monthly wage in 1920 for a local worker was between 180 and 200 pesetas) and touring South America, he always suffered from poverty.

THE FRANCOIST REGIME: VAGRANTS, CRIMINALS AND THE GAYEST OASIS IN THE DESERT

When the Spanish Civil War erupted in 1936 the cabaret and entertainment industry plummeted, and most intellectuals and artists who would not align themselves with the national Catholic ideology were forced to hide or flee to France, or risk imprisonment. General Francisco Franco took over the country in a totalitarian dictatorship supported by the Catholic Church. In 1954 the regime modified the law concerning vagrants and criminals to define any form of homosexual behaviour as a crime.

Every form of queer expression by necessity became clandestine, censored or non-existent, but there were some queens, such as Madame Arthur in Barcelona, who kept the cabaret scene alive. Franco invested in propaganda to put forward his view of Spanish identity, and exaggerated

BELOW: Manolita Chen opening Madrid's LGBTIQ+ Pride of 2023: 'We must fight for our dignity and respect. In 1983 I became the first trans woman to possess a female ID and to adopt five children. Pride doesn't happen only on June 28th, we must fight for it each and every day.'

and industrialized Andalusian folklore, the Catholic religion and traditions linked to it. Rosario Molina, a queen of the Andalusian drag house Las Niñas (The Girls), tells us about drag during Francoism:

> *They took a lot of inspiration from the* copla *and* cuplé *musical genres. Something curious about this inspiration is how hard it was to get any products from overseas: you had to get them at the military bases, which no queer person would approach. So the only thing they had was our national products.*

The regime also invested in the hotel industry as a way to cope with the war debt, so Torremolinos, a small fishing town on the southern coast, underwent a tourism boom in the late 1950s and started to attract international icons. The city quickly became one of the country's first LGBTQ+ hubs, even in the midst of the dictatorship, and Spain's first gay and lesbian bars opened there. This oasis of gayness and liberty in the middle of the desert also hosted Manolita Chen, the first legally trans person in Spain, who worked as a vedette in Pasaje Begoña, an alley known for its prevalence of gay bars.

In 1970, however, the 'Law Concerning Vagrants and Criminals' was modified to become the 'Law Concerning Social Danger and Rehabilitation', and the following year the party was over in Torremolinos. In June 1971, in what became known as the Great Raid, police closed all

> "Just as drag queens in the United States enjoyed to impersonate their Hollywood divas, our queens impersonated our folkloric divas."

the gay bars and arrested more than 100 people. Unlike the Stonewall riots in New York City in 1969, this incident permanently stopped all gay activity in the city until the late 2010s, when Torremolinos revived its drag scene with Pride parades and other parties.

'FRANCO HA MUERTO': FOLKLORIC CAMPINESS, COUNTERCULTURE AND CLUBS

During the final years of Franco's dictatorship, drag started to reanimate, as the drag queen La Caneli explains:

> *[Andalusian] folklore was our main source of culture throughout the twentieth century, and just as drag queens in the United States liked to impersonate their Hollywood divas, ours impersonated our folkloric divas: Lola Flores, Rocío Jurado, Concha Piquer … In fact, when the movie* Cabaret *premiered here, each and every travesti prepared their own Liza [Minnelli] number with a bobbed wig and a chair. It was an epidemic.*

José Pérez Ocaña, a Sevillian painter from a humble background, brought his southern traditions to the scene in Barcelona. He did whatever he wanted, wherever he wanted: singing to the Virgin Mary the way only

women could do (he was a fervent Catholic); walking the famous street La Rambla during the day while wearing women's clothing, followed by an intrigued crowd of locals to whom he would flash his penis; or performing *coplas* in cemeteries while in drag.

Despite all this, Ocaña didn't define himself as a drag queen. His only goal was to provoke and manifest his art, to perform his own gender expression and faith in ways that no man could do under a Catholic regime. He suffered from AIDS, and, after he accidentally set fire to his costume during a performance, his condition worsened until his death in September 1983. To this day, Ocaña's art and persona are symbols for drag and gender non-conforming communities.

Drag had lost its status, and had turned dark and obscene, often consisting of stripteases in front of a curious audience. Paco España dominated the scene as an impersonator, and there was also La Esmeralda, from Seville, who loved coarse humour and used to say 'I'm a FAGGOT, with your mouth wide open, like in VAAAAULT.'

Franco's death in 1975 began the transition to democracy. Madrid became the centre of the drag scene with the Movida Madrileña, a countercultural movement of a liberated generation. Valencia also burst on to the scene with the Ruta del Bacalao, a tour of never-ending parties and free-flowing drugs, with such queens as Miss Nacha Boheme as dancers.

ABOVE: Drag Sethlas during his provocative performance in Las Palmas Carnival of 2017, which unleashed the outrage of religious groups.

Cabaret and *coplas* slowly shifted to disco and techno during the 1980s, and drag culture was led by Psicosis Gonsales and Paco España. Queens turned into a disco ball of glitter and feathers that illuminated the entire party; they mingled with other LGBTQ+ advocates of the Movida, such as the film director Pedro Almodóvar and TV personality El Gran Wyoming, and made their first appearances on music videos and television. The pop singer Alaska even had her own entourage of 'court ladies' (drag queens) for her tours.

During this period of liberation, queer people reappropriated folklore and religion, the symbols of the patriarchal culture imposed by Franco. La Petróleo y La Salvaora, an artistic flamenco duet of drag queens and trans women, performed in the *tablaos* (flamenco venues) of Spain and ended up touring the United States in 1986, with Lola Flores.

It is important to keep in mind that Spain went from being an overwhelmingly Catholic country, in which the Church had a strong influence in the state's organisation, to being a country where almost 40 per cent of the population identify as atheist, in only sixty years. Folklore and religion have left an enormous, satirical footprint in Spanish drag. Plenty of drag queens not only parody and exaggerate (*campify*) the Spanish image that emerged from that time, but also celebrate them, just as Ocaña celebrated his Andalusian roots and his faith in Barcelona.

During the Canarian Drag Gala in 2017, for example, Drag Sethlas performed Madonna's song 'Like a Prayer' dressed as a Holy Week Virgin Mary statue, before transforming into Jesus Christ hanging on the Cross, and emulating the Last Supper. He was subsequently sued for blasphemy by a Christian association of lawyers, a case that echoed throughout the media.

CANARIAN DRAG: HIGH BOOTS, CROWDED VENUES AND GREAT EXPECTATIONS

In the late 1990s a journalist in the Canary Islands conceived of a project to include the boundary-breaking drag-queen movement in the islands' biggest touristic event: the Las Palmas Carnival. This Drag Gala was seen as posing a risk to the success of the Carnival, and the outcome was hard to predict; there would be a televised drag contest, live performances and a final crowning of the queen of the festival. After some consideration, the organizers took the risk and celebrated the first Drag Gala of Las Palmas.

Pepe Naranjo, writer for the journal *Canarias7*, described the gala as follows:

A real show. Youngsters with a lewd attitude, sheathed in their funny costumes – although some showed more skin than they hid – overflowing with feathers and sequins, twirling around the stage. And a dedicated audience for this gala, which may have been simple, but which had the right ingredients to become, in time, one of the most eagerly awaited acts of the entire Carnival.

The style of the Canarian artists differs from any other. They wear platforms 40 cm (15 in) tall, and nudity is very welcome. Rhinestones and huge headpieces with fantasy make-up abound. Performers are surrounded by a body of dancers, also in drag for the night.

The Drag Gala wasn't a small show in the darkness of a little suburban bar, but an outstanding televised success that more than 7,000 people came to watch in person. RuPaul visited in 2008, a year before the premiere of *RuPaul's Drag Race*, and the tradition lives on.

Y2K: POP SENSATIONS AND TV MOMENTS

"Celebrity impersonators became less popular as queens created their own style."

The film *The Adventures of Priscilla, Queen of the Desert* (1994) changed plenty of drag wardrobes in Spain, bringing neon and platinum, crazy wigs and over-the-top make-up. No longer effeminate and simplistic, drag came closer to the hyperbolic shows we are used to watching today. Spain joined the EU in 1986, and hosted the Olympic Games in 1992, for the first time in history, when Freddie Mercury and the Spanish operatic soprano Montserrat Caballé sang 'Barcelona' together. Over just a very few years Spain had taken steps towards modernity, and opened its shell to the rest of the world.

More drag arrived on television in commercials, music, interviews … Even Almodóvar asked a drag queen (Sandra Montiel) to appear in his movie *Bad Education* (2004). La Prohibida, Supremme de Luxe, Deborah Ombres, Kika Lorace, Pupi Poisson and other queens invaded public consciousness gently with their pop music.

Celebrity impersonators became less popular as queens created their own style. Drag queens and other artistic personas became even more popular on mainstream television: La Veneno on trashy chat shows and Deborah Ombres as an anchor on *MTV Hot* or a host of *Caiga quien Caiga*.

An important personality at this time was Miss Shangay Lily, who used her platform for advocating for LGBTQ+ rights and was a strong critic of 'gaypitalism', the use of queer identities for business. Particularly memorable was her interruption of a meeting of the Popular Party in 2010, in full drag with turban and tunic, screaming against homophobia in the party. She also had a cameo with Javier Bardem in the movie *Boca a Boca* (*Mouth to Mouth*; 1995), made her own film (*Santa Miguel de Molina*, 2005) and applied for the Eurovision Song Contest in 2008 with the electro hit 'HiperSuperMegaDiva', a year after the Ukrainian drag persona Verka Serduchka had taken second place with 'Dancing Lasha Tumbai'.

With the beginning of social media, Pupi Poisson released her (in) famous song 'Putón Verbenero' (Party Slut), a gleeful parody of a rumba

recorded in 1962 by Manolo Escobar and Sara Montiel. La Prohibida started her music career, releasing her first electro pop album, Flash, in 2005 and touring Europe and South America.

The internet made it easier to cross-dress and fight stigma thanks to the sharing of fashion and make-up tips. Still, even in the early twenty-first century Spain was quite old-fashioned and intolerant. Drag was celebrated only in the darkest corners of the brightest cities. But that decade brought a shift in drag, the creation of new spaces in which to participate and be visible, to be hungry and say, 'I'm right here, *maricon* [faggot]!'

A NEW GENERATION: POLKA-DOTTED DIVAS AND ANIME MONSTERS

ABOVE: Samantha Hudson in her tour 'Liquidación Total' ('Clearance Sale'). One of the most recognizable faces of Spanish camp performance, and currently a trash and hyperpop music singer.

The latest generation of drag queens has been heavily influenced by television culture – that of both Spanish and American shows – and the references have diversified. Drag kings and monsters have started to make an appearance, too.

A good part of the present generation of queers grew up with Japanese anime, such as *Cardcaptor Sakura*, *Crayon Shin-Chan* and *One Piece*,

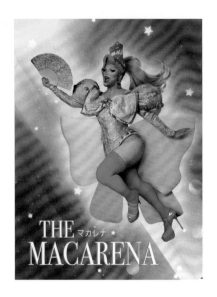

THE マカレナ
MACARENA

especially on Andalusia's television channels. That is why the queens of this generation incorporate anime and video games into their drag: they make their outfits following their favourite video game's concept art; they sing the opening theme of a popular show; and they incorporate jokes from much-loved childhood movies into their routines. Some of them started out with cosplay before turning to drag.

Most recently, thanks to drag's leap into the mainstream, it has diversified into parties, concerts, theatre, new television shows and day drag. The concept of the Dragalada Drag Tour has spread across Spanish cities like wildfire: an afternoon show during which guests are guided to various bars, in each of which a queen awaits with their number. This format has allowed queer people to demonstrate to their friends and family how fun and varied drag can be, and to challenge the misconception that it is all about nightclubs and stripping. Shows have also shifted from not requiring the audience to pay much attention to the queen in the background, to 'sit and watch' drag that takes over theatrical spaces. Now, every gay club in every city wants its own drag queen.

TRAVESTIS AND MARICONES: REAPPROPIATING THE PAST

I always say that my drag is a mix between the Andalusian [comedy] group Los Morancos and a Bratz doll.

Rosario Molina

The Spanish brand of drag consists of sharp satire and wit, parties, clubs, fun, pop, television references and, of course, sorting all gender norms into the *travesti* identity – a slur that predominated in Spanish society, and one that queens and kings have made their own. They reappropriated the polka dots, sequins, ruffled skirts and wooden fans that boys – and, to a certain extent, girls – were for so long forbidden from wearing. There's plenty of room for fake lashes and lipstick, but there's room too for those clowns and beasts that are lurking in our bars, looking out for us, and ensuring that we have a safe space and an unforgettable night.

Hasta luego, ¡maricón!

ABOVE: The Macarena's entrance look for the first season of *Drag Race España*: a look mixing the animated magical girl attire with elements from flamenco.

OPPOSITE: Performance of the drag house 'Las Niñas' held in the Reina Sofia Art Museum in Madrid in 2023.

THE NORDIC ROYAL FAMILIES

Viktor 'Caffeine' Skancke

Like many countries, Sweden is a smorgasbord of drag.
The Swedish created the word, after all, for different dishes coming together to create a feast. This art form has gone from being totally unappreciated by the majority to being a controversial political subject loved by the public; from being simply all about female impersonation to encompassing unlimited ways of creating art and performances. Drag performers in Sweden have a history of being pack animals.

PREVIOUS PAGE: Elecktra, member of
Cabaret Moulin and third-runner up in
the first season of *Drag Race Sverige*.

FEMALE IMPERSONATION AND QUESTION MARKS

One of the earliest Swedish drag performers was John Lindström, better
known as John Lind and sometimes styled with two question marks as
'?Lind?'. The stage name was a joking connection to the Swedish soprano
Jenny Lind, the question marks symbolizing the 'confusion' over which
Lind was which. One of the most internationally famous Swedish
performers before the First World War, ?Lind? toured the world for more
than twenty years in the twentieth century, returning to Sweden in 1923.

At the time, female impersonation was not appreciated in Sweden,
so ?Lind? performed there only once, despite international success. The
acts were inspired by the five senses. ?Lind? impersonated famous female
figures from history, performed pastiches of famous female dancers, and
sang opera (another connection to the soprano Lind), all while dressed
flamboyantly in the height of chic, with corsets, dresses and big hats.
The idea was to present the illusion of a strong female, from look to
performance, and to confuse and fascinate the audience, to make them
question whether it was a man or a woman in the dress.

IT'S JUST THEATRE

Drag, or rather female impersonation, became more common in Swedish
variety theatre during the first half of the twentieth century in the form of
small sketches, when male performers would play a female character for
one number. These were not really drag queens by name or trade, but such
sketches encouraged an acceptance of the joy in playing with gender for
the purpose of entertainment. The legendary revue performer Lasse Krantz
became popular in Stockholm with his pastiches of such icons as Greta
Garbo, Zarah Leander and Karin Kavli. The fame he gained for these acts
was so great that in 1940 he starred in a television commercial for the
shaving cream Hylins Rakin, which he maintained was so good that it left
his skin perfectly smooth for his drag performances. The main character in
the film *Fram för lilla Märta* (*March Forward for Lil' Miss Märta*; 1945)
took on a female persona, and the movie received excellent reviews.
However, the art of drag was still seen as a tool for male actors to create
comedy characters within their repertoire. These were characters
performed by (at least outwardly) straight men for whom drag was just
that, a character, and the transformation just for the stage.

ABOVE: Stig Järrel as the cellist Sture
Letterström, impersonating as his female
alter ego, the cellist and later politician,
Märta.

IT'S ALWAYS BRIGHTER AFTER DARK

It was not until the 1970s that drag performed by queer people started to
blossom, and the art form of changing gender for entertainment began to

? LIND ?

ABOVE: A poster promoting one of ?Lind?'s shows.

be labelled 'drag'. On the nightlife scene, queens would strut around with padded bras, pearl earrings and large wigs. These big ladies – big glamorous ladies – would mingle, perform, make people laugh and impersonate celebrities. They took drag down from the stage and out into the world. In the bubbling party era of 1976, one group started a venue that would become drag legend. Christer Lindarw, Lasse Flinckman and Roger Jönsson opened Club After Dark in Stockholm. As After Dark they became a popular pub show and got their big break in 1980 performing at the music bar Hamburger Börs, a stage that many Swedish performers – and even the likes of Frank Sinatra and Liza Minnelli – have graced. Jönsson left the group in 1981 to start the more provocative drag group Surprise Sisters, which took over After Dark's spot at its eponymous club.

While After Dark focused on a glittering, glamorous lip-syncing style of drag, Surprise Sisters focused on provocation, nerve and comedy. The latter eventually took their act abroad, while After Dark stayed in Sweden for forty-two years, disbanding in 2018 before being revived with a new ensemble in 2022. During this time, as far as the Swedish population was concerned, After Dark became the face of drag, competing in 2004 in Melodifestivalen (the Melody Festival), a six-week-long Saturday-night television competition to determine the song that would represent Sweden in the Eurovision Song Contest. Despite not winning, After Dark's song 'La Dolce Vita' became a big hit. Since Melodifestivalen is a family-friendly show that brings all generations together to watch it, After Dark's entry became the first experience of drag performance for many children and young people. It showed them that drag exists and even inspired some to try it themselves. Flinckman retired from drag in 2009 and passed away in 2016. Lindarw, described by the press as 'the most beautiful woman in Sweden' for his style of drag, came out of retirement as a producer for the revival of After Dark. This gained traction in the news, keeping After Dark in the public consciousness as the face of drag.

DRAGS OF A FEATHER, STICK TOGETHER

During the 1990s, when alternative clubs began popping up, and when a venue might be open one week and replaced the next by something new, drag continued to be a party uniform. It was not uncommon to perform drag as a group in Sweden, and many performers were known better as part of a group than by their drag name – if they even had one. During this decade and the early 2000s, various drag groups were on the rise. The Diamond Dogs, for example, specialized in parody re-recordings of hit pop songs. The high-tempo dance group Drag-On-Line and the costumey comedy group Fashion Pack, along with many others, were also popular.

Instead of creating a persona, drag concentrated on female and celebrity impersonation in a similar way to past – often straight – revue

performers in the sense that the focus was on the illusion and the act. One exception was Babsan, a founding member of Surprise Sisters. Unlike the sisters from her drag generation, she became known as her character, with her signature pink wig, pink dress ... well, pink everything! She became a stalwart on television as the host of her own shows, a few of them aimed at children, showing that her bubblegum-tinged enthusiasm for glamour could suit all generations.

While still known under his legal name, Lars-Åke Wilhelmsson, the character Babsan became known as her own person. It was something like the beloved character Tiffany Persson, performed by the comedian Anders Jansson, who played several fictional characters in the sketch show Hipp Hipp! Whether Tiffany is a drag queen or 'just' a female impersonation has been a subject of discussion, but what is agreed is that she's a creation from the art of drag. She even received the Drag Queen of the Year award at the Gaygala in 2004. With that and After Dark's performance in Melodifestivalen, drag stepped out from the clubs and bar shows into the living rooms of the Swedish population.

For the Swedish public, drag became more connected to glamour, beauty and soft femininity, as well as theatre, comedy and powerful ladies. But for the people of the nightlife and club scene, drag remained less easy

ABOVE: After Dark competing with their song 'La Dolce Vita', 2004. Flinckman is on the the left and Lindarw on the right.

OPPOSITE: Babsan in her signature pink on her tour 'Ett liv i rosa', in Sweden in 2017.

to define. A group that carried the flag for more edgy drag was Cunigunda, founded by former After Dark members who wanted to switch the sequins for plastic, neon and heavy bass music. Perhaps their most famous member is Robert Fux, the host of *Drag Race Sverige*.

With Babsan, Tiffany Persson and After Dark performing in almost everyone's living room in the mid-2000s, a new generation of drag performers grew up seeing drag and being inspired. Female impersonation remains a staple of theatre culture and drag groups are still formed, but individuality has become more of a focus and more performers now have their own drag names. Although they are still popular, drag groups are presented more as a collective of individuals than as an ensemble. This is partially because of social media, which allows individual drag performers to promote and present their own drag instead of having to rely on the marketing of a group.

FINDING HEEL-STAMPING GROUNDS

With gentrification and increasing rents, venues have begun to struggle and disappear. In the 1990s the number of venues gave access for clubs to start up easily. Some just lasted a weekend, but through that a club culture

"[Babsan's] bubblegum-tinged enthusiasm for glamour could suit all generations."

PREVIOUS PAGE: Drag king Qarl Qunt performing on his national tour 'Slick'.

OPPOSITE: The legendary drag group Cunigunda.

would be formed, centred more around the people than the club itself. Even so, Swedish drag performers are investigating new possibilities and finding creative solutions, among them underground clubs, theatre stages and drag brunches.

Gothenburg, Sweden's second-largest city, has declined from its position as the party city of the 1990s. The once numerous venues, especially queer ones, are steadily disappearing, so the younger generation of drag performers are taking their art back to underground clubs. Gothenburg's drag has become more influenced by genderfuck and punk aesthetics and ideals. Using unconventional materials – fishnet stockings stuffed with balloons as a wig, for example – drag performers are more creatures than kings and queens, challenging gender and celebrating queer joy. This isn't unique or new in the country, but Gothenburg is certainly a creative city for drag that pushes boundaries and celebrates queerness, even if you have to put your ear to the ground to find it.

The venues in Malmö, Sweden's third-largest city, have also suffered the effects of gentrification and a slow economy. With Copenhagen just a short train ride away, though, and as host of the annual charity event Dragshowgalan (on hiatus at time of writing) Malmö remains a Nordic hotspot for classic, glamorous drag. Queer venues are popping up slowly, but drag is also finally public enough to be featured at non-queer venues, such as Moriska Paviljongen, where the group Cabaret Moulin takes the stage. It seems that in Malmö drag has a sequin-bright future.

Drag can be found in cities of all sizes, and even out in the woods in small towns like Mora, but the main drag hive remains Stockholm. For generations, this has been the city for young queers from small towns to move to, and it still is. Stockholm has given countless people room to dream and live. Queer venues have stayed, but not without a fight against gentrification and the damage to nightlife caused by people moving into the city and complaining about noise to such an extent that businesses are forced to close. Even so, Stockholm drag always finds a stage to walk on. It has fought to find and keep ground on which to perform and be creative, sometimes claiming and sharing that space with the world of ballroom. In this international city with deep queer roots, drag is influenced strongly by global trends, although it still honours the familiar comedic, glamorous drag.

SOMETHING OLD, SOMETIMES NEW, ALWAYS DRAG, YELLOW AND BLUE

Female impersonation has faded out of style in drag, but celebrity impersonation remains a staple. It is still one of the most popular drag forms with the general public, probably another effect of After Dark's success, since celebrity impersonation was one of their signatures before and after their revival. Anton Engström's celebrity impressions – of the

> "Rebels and queers create ways to express themselves ... carrying on their elders' legacy with punkyavant-garde, alien-inspired performances and celebrity impressions."

television host Tilde de Paula Eby and the politician Annie Lööf, among many others – became popular enough to spring him from the stage of Club After Dark to perform on television and become a sought-after guest on chat shows and radio programmes.

Although much loved, drag has been under attack in Sweden, just as it has in other countries. Far-right politicians decry it as perverse, especially questioning drag that caters for children, such as reading children's books in libraries or providing guided tours in theatres. Most of these arguments are copied-and-pasted from those made by United States' Republican politicians, but it has come to a point where the leaders of all Swedish political parties have had public debates on the subject. The politician Jan Jönsson showed his personal support and took a stance by being put in drag and reading books to children in Stockholm, making the statement that drag can be for everyone – it's just a question of how it is packaged. An art form that has historically been widely accepted and beloved has suddenly become the subject of tense discussion, needing to be defended against accusations of immorality. Once again, drag performers have to be protectors of their queer community.

For a long time in Sweden, the drag queen – that is to say, a man dressing up as a woman – was the only form of drag that people thought of. But as drag becomes a tool for expression and playing with gender, more eyes turn to Swedish drag kings as they begin to get the recognition they deserve. A fun piece of trivia is the fact that the Swedish for drag queen is *druga* (plural *drugor*). No one really knows where the word came from, besides being a Swedishification of the word drag. It's possible that the 'a' in drag became a 'u' because drag in Swedish means 'pull'. The word has nothing to do with drugs.

In the Swedish drag scene, rebels and queers create ways to express themselves and be free, carrying on their elders' legacy with punky avant-garde, outer space alien-inspired performances and celebrity impressions, entertaining children as clownish characters, or being glamorous, beautiful, funny women. Like Admira Thunderpussy. Like Christer Lindarw. Like ?Lind?. In the end, Swedes just love glamour and having a laugh.

ABOVE: Anton Engström (left), former member of the revived After Dark, posing as and together with politician Annie Lööf (right).

OPPOSITE: Artist duo Status Queer at Gothenburg underground club SJUKT.

A PANTO-DWELLING, DEEPLY POLITICAL DRAG HISTORY

Zephyr Aspen

It's a safe bet that the first drag experience of anyone growing up in the UK will be pantomime. A beloved festive tradition, pantos are interactive, immersive retellings of children's fairy tales packed with slapstick gags, garish costumes and sneaky innuendo to make the parents chuckle. Within this fail-safe formula, there's always at least one drag role, and it's almost inevitably the male lead's mother – you probably know her as the pantomime dame.

While men who play pantomime dames don't always consider themselves drag queens, there are similarities in their histories. The first and most obvious link is that they're both traditionally men dressed in women's clothing, but there's also the fact that both craft their names from clever puns (such as England's own Ella Vaday).

Seemingly, pantomime history is influenced by the ancient Roman-inspired pagan custom in which a peasant became the 'Lord of Misrule' every December. This temporary figure was put in charge of entertainment for the annual feast, a responsibility that entailed role reversal and general merriment. Pantomime borrows from this history of gender-swapping; men play the dames, and women often play the young male protagonist – the 'principal boy' – such as Jack in *Jack and the Beanstalk*.

According to researchers from the Victoria and Albert Museum in London, the structure of panto is derived from the Italian *commedia dell'arte* that toured Europe from the sixteenth century onwards. These shows featured many roles that are familiar from panto today, such as the harlequin character, a precursor of the dame. By the eighteenth century

PREVIOUS PAGE: Actor Joe Meloy as pantomime character Widow Twankey in *A Lad in Tights*.

RIGHT: A painting depicting characters from the *commedia dell'arte* era, including harlequins, clowns and a principal dancer.

OPPOSITE: Phylip Harries (Widow Twankey) and Alex Parry (Abanazer) in *Aladdin The Wok n Roll Panto* at the Theatr Clwyd in Mold, Wales in 2010.

these archetypes were omnipresent in London's theatres, which at the time were presenting classical stories with no dialogue. The evolution of panto began in the early nineteenth century, when the manager of the Drury Lane Theatre became the first to give the harlequin spoken lines, either narrating known stories or ones written specially for the show.

Changes kept coming. The 1830s brought the introduction of special effects, and dialogue restrictions – put in place by the prime minister Robert Warpole in 1737 as a censorship measure – were lifted in 1843. Before long, panto was defined – as it still is today – by jokes, wordplay and hilarious social satire. In this period, panto consolidated its contemporary festive formula, generally opening for its run on Boxing Day. Better yet, unlike other forms of theatre, pantos weren't solely for the middle classes; tiered ticket prices and performances in heavily working-class towns nationwide meant that these cheeky, cross-dressing extravaganzas were relatively easy to access.

Nowadays, 'adult pantos' give the tradition a life beyond Christmas, working the draggiest elements of panto – wit, camp humour, live singing and bold personas – into raunchy, rip-roaring 18+ shows. Led by such charismatic British queens as Sophia Stardust and Divina de Campo, these adult pantos remain a must-see.

SHAKESPEARE'S SUCH A DRAG

Nobody can agree on how the term 'drag' first came into use, but it is agreed that it was coined in the UK. Some describe it as folk etymology derived from theatre slang. The *Online Etymology Dictionary* suggests the term was used as early as 1870, a reference to 'the sensation of long skirts trailing on the floor', and proposes that 'another guess is Yiddish *trogn* "to wear", from German *tragen*.' It is a popular myth that 'drag' was a Shakespearean acronym for 'dressed resembling a girl' or 'dressed as a girl', but there is no proof of that. What we *do* know is that – according to *By Arcadia* – 'drag queen' was first used to describe men appearing in women's clothing in Polari, a queer British slang popularized among gay men and the theatre community in the late nineteenth and twentieth centuries.

Drag is often traced back to Shakespearean theatre, but these origins aren't exactly progressive; at the time, the Church of England ruled that no AFAB performers were allowed on the stage. This meant that any 'female'

ABOVE: Le Gateau Chocolat dazzles in gold onstage at the Globe Theatre in a Studio 54 inspired take on *Twelfth Night*, May 2017.

OPPOSITE: A mid-eighteenth century image of a molly house, meeting places for gay men often frequented by Princess Seraphina.

roles *must* be played by a man, including roles depicting famous figures, such as Cleopatra. There's evidence of women transgressing these limitations, and in 2018 *The Guardian* newspaper published an article detailing their lives and the stigma they faced. Merely being an female actor on the stage would result in you being branded a 'whore', and it was reported that wealthy men would offer extra cash to watch the women get changed before the show. Theatre companies wrote disclaimers warning the audience that real women were due to feature on the stage that night, and the actor and poet Thomas Jordan even wrote a letter promising that an actress wasn't a 'whore' – a charming endorsement!

Luckily, today's theatre is more progressive, and drag artists often take inspiration from the work of Shakespeare. The drag star Le Gateau Chocolat, for example – whose children's show *Duckie* (first presented in 2016) taught kids about otherness and self-acceptance – played Feste in *Twelfth Night* at the hallowed Globe Theatre in London in 2017. In 2023 the Globe showed *If It Please You*, an amalgamation of readings, performance and conversation brought to life through drag. The show was curated by the drag king Nina Bowers and Isabel Adomakoh Young, founding member of the all-female/non-binary drag king theatre and cabaret company Pecs Drag Kings, established in 2013. These trailblazers are name-checking and subverting Shakespeare's theatre, bringing the history of drag to new audiences.

THE ONE WHO STARTED IT ALL?

A little-known chapter of Britain's LGBTQ+ history is that of the early eighteenth-century 'molly houses' where 'mollies' – gay men – would meet to drink booze, crack jokes and maybe even hook up. It was in these fabled houses that John Cooper, a gentleman's servant, perfected his glamorous alter ego Princess Seraphina, perhaps the first drag queen in the UK. Seraphina was a molly-house regular throughout the eighteenth century, but, despite many raids by the authorities, she was never arrested.

In fact, Seraphina dealt with the courts just once – as prosecutor, not defendant. She took a thief to court after he stole her clothes, and although she didn't win the case, testimony from local women who were washerwomen and pub landladies, reveals that she was referred to using she/her pronouns both in and out of drag. In their statements, the women marvel at her style, beauty and exemplary elegance. 'She would so flutter her fan, and make such fine curtsies, that you would not have known her from a woman,' said Mary Poplet, who described Seraphina's signature look: 'a white gown and a scarlet cloak, with her hair frizzled and curled all around her forehead.' It's reassuring that, for once, a historical example of drag excellence was seemingly met with praise, respect and acceptance.

A MORNING FROLIC, or the TRANSMUTATION of SEXES.

DANNY LA RUE: DRAG ON STAGE

After the Second World War, there was still reluctance to accept the LGBTQ+ community. Despite this, some drag acts made a splash in the 1950s and 60s, and Danny La Rue (1927–2009) was one of them. At school, his baby-faced good looks 'often meant he was cast as a girl in school plays', and when he entered the Navy in 1944, at just seventeen years old, he even joined the ship's concert troupe, 'playing a native girl in a comic send-up of [the recent film] *White Cargo*'. For years afterwards, he continued to play roles written for women. La Rue was later offered a short-term slot at the Churchill Bar in London, 'which became a three-year engagement as top of the bill'. He followed this with a seven-year run at Winston's, 'and in March 1964 he opened his eponymous nightclub in Hanover Square', which 'attracted royalty, celebrities and the general public', and is said to have had as many as 13,000 members at one time. His acts often involved impersonating those who inspired much of the 'vogue' movement, such as Marlene Dietrich and Elizabeth Taylor.

La Rue 'always insisted that his act was in no way sexually subversive or ground-breaking, and that he was not a drag queen but just "a bloke in a frock" who dressed up for laughs'. Such statements are revealing of society's attitude to drag at the time, showing that this art form was occasionally accepted as part of the mainstream, but only when it was politically tame. La Rue made his television debut in 1958, and soon became a regular fixture; within ten years, he was one of Britain's most popular stars. He even made it on to the silver screen, playing a drag queen in Second World War France in *Our Miss Fred* (1972), and in 1984 he became the first man to take a leading female role in a major West End production with his star turn in *Hello, Dolly*! La Rue was an advocate, too; following the death of his partner Wayne King to the virus in 2000, he fundraised tirelessly for AIDS charities, earning Queen Elizabeth II's recognition in 2002 in the form of the prestigious OBE.

RADICAL DRAG

While La Rue was finding success, activists of the UK's Gay Liberation Front were using 'radical drag' to make bold queer political statements. They dragged up as nuns to take aim at evangelical homophobia, and in 1971 protestors donned dresses and wigs and brandished placards outside a London court as feminist campaigners were put on trial for flour-bombing the 1970 'Miss World' pageant, decrying it as a 'cattle market' that objectified women.

Especially in the UK, class has played a key role in drag history. Working-class queer artists, such as David Hoyle and Bette Bourne, revelled in creating drag personas with outspoken leftist views and a

ramshackle approach to costume design. They favoured a deliberately DIY aesthetic, and Bourne's Bloolips troupe, for example, famously used everything from mopheads to charity-shop bric-a-brac to put their looks together. If drag was growing more radical in the late 1970s, the 1980s and the global spread of the AIDS crisis accelerated this political shift. People were pissed off, and drag quickly came to represent that fury.

Enter Lily Savage, the drag persona of the British television legend Paul O'Grady. A foul-mouthed sex worker with a towering blonde beehive, working-class roots and an acid tongue, Lily took inspiration from working-class women. Often dressed from head to toe in animal print with wipe-clean high-heeled boots, she was renowned for her sharp wit and exceptional hosting skills on stage and on television, although she had had a long, gruelling rise through the queer club scenes of Manchester, Liverpool and London. Famously, one of her stand-up gigs at London's Royal Vauxhall Tavern in 1987 was raided by police wearing rubber gloves; AIDS misinformation was rife at the time, so there was fear that merely touching the surfaces of a gay bar would result in infection. Unfazed, Lily quipped: 'Well well, looks like we've got help with the washing up!' O'Grady retired Lily in 2004, feeling she didn't fit into modern times, but he continued to perform in drag for the rest of his career, in musicals and pantomimes. His drag talent, quick wit and charitable work cemented his reputation as a national treasure and a true working-class hero, the kind of down-to-earth, politically conscious drag star who exemplified the best of British drag.

DRAGGING ITS WAY KICKING AND SCREAMING TO STAGE AND TV

Since the turn of the millennium British drag has slowly crept into the mainstream, creating household names in the process. Jamie Campbell, the real-life star behind the hit musical *Everybody's Talking about Jamie* (first presented in 2017), was a drag queen by the age of sixteen and battled with his school to be allowed to attend his prom in a dress. Campbell has without a doubt played a part in bringing queer politics – including the politics of drag – into mainstream discussion, appearing on news shows to speak about the often hostile reality of being a young queer person doing drag. He has since gravitated away from drag and towards fashion, and he explained this choice in an interview with *i-D* magazine in 2020:

Drag has grown in popularity so fast, but it is a double-edged sword ... I think it's amazing that so many people are accepting of it and being exposed to it, but then, as with anything that becomes commercial, it gets watered down a bit. The standard of drag is so high now – everybody's

ABOVE: Lily Savage (Paul O'Grady) on stage in a custom outfit inspired by Grace Jones.

OPPOSITE: Danny La Rue as Dolly in *Hello Dolly!* in London's West End, 1984.

just so good — and with me not doing it as often, I felt like my drag was not where I wanted it to be either … I was putting out things that I wasn't necessarily happy with and because of Drag Race and the internet, everybody has become a critic. When really? They don't have a clue what goes into being a drag queen.

PREVIOUS PAGE: Pecs Drag Kings, the all-female/non-binary drag king theatre and cabaret company.

ABOVE: With his bold makeup and working-class background, Manchester's David Hoyle has blended visual arts and cabaret with the avant-garde across film and TV since the 1980s, unafraid to present pieces on mental health, AIDS, revolution and other pressing political and difficult issues.

OPPOSITE: Jamie Campbell at the premiere for *Everybody's Talking About Jamie*, Sheffield, 2021.

Everybody's Talking about Jamie gave British audiences the gift of a heartfelt portrayal of drag and queerness, but not all mainstream brushes with drag have been so progressive. In the early 2000s, comedians David Walliams and Matt Lucas created the wildly popular sketch show *Little Britain*, crafting a handful of cross-dressing personas to make sketches about daily life in the UK. There was Emily, an 'unconvincing transvestite' played by Walliams, whose masculinity becomes a constant target for jokes. Unsurprisingly, Emily is never acknowledged as a woman, and the gags always lie in her failure to perform femininity 'convincingly'. Then there's Vicky Pollard, a school-age Bristolian who exemplifies the 'chav' label used to demean working-class people. In the show, Pollard is envious of a nine-year-old who already has three children and her own council house. In one scene, Pollard swaps her baby for a Westlife CD and works as a sex-line operator, where she pretends to be a lesbian. In the US version of the show, she expresses concern to her school coach that one of her classmates is a lesbian, despite having pretended to be one herself.

The show has been retrospectively met with backlash (so much so that one of the only remaining sources of information about it is Wikipedia), not just for its stereotyping of gay and trans people, but also for its use of blackface. These characters don't embody the ethos of drag as a gloriously queer, subversive art form, but they do prove that drag can be used to punch down at marginalized communities – and, in the case of *Little Britain*, audiences eat this up.

UK HUN?

The UK drag scene was truly catapulted into the mainstream with the arrival of *RuPaul's Drag Race UK*, but the show's success has had its downsides. Although it is not always the case, the franchise has been criticized for favouring a specific form of high-femme drag, and as a result, performers who don't fit this aesthetic can have a harder time getting booked or recognized. The show platforms drag queens only, which makes it hard for drag kings, non-binary/androgynous drag performers, drag 'things' and 'monsters' to get bookings. As always, there are exceptions – the successful West End show *Death Drop* (which first opened in 2020) brought together a range of drag performers and truly foregrounded drag kings – but the disproportionate spotlight that is shone on Drag Race makes it hard for less conventional performers to thrive.

On the other hand, drag in the UK is broader and more diverse than ever before. Drag monsters, such as Sheffield's King Confuza, Glasgow's Puke and Manchester's BollyWitch, are consistently pushing boundaries, whereas collectives such as the Cocoa Butter Club and nights like Sheffield's Andro & Eve and London's Magic Mike are creating space and platforms for under-represented performers.

There's a great deal that sets the UK's drag scene apart. Because of its roots in pantomime, British drag is captivating, fun and all-round *camp*. Many performers sing live during their sets, nodding to drag's rich theatrical history, but drag varies depending on where in the UK you are. In big cities, you might see high-energy, explosive numbers in crowded nightclubs. Travel to the coast and you'll find the likes of Blackpool, a working-class seaside town with a penchant for glitz and glamour that attracts more 'old-school' and comedy drag. Cabaret-style shows dominate the UK drag scene, even in smaller cities, such as Leeds. In Wales, the Millennium Centre in Cardiff opened a cabaret stage in February 2023 and regularly features drag artists; in Scotland, scripted shows and reimaginations of musicals are vastly popular, with between four and eight drag artists involved in each one. The drag scene is booming, and performers across the country continue to innovate and delight their audiences, nodding to the UK's campy, distinctly working-class drag identity as they do so.

"Because of its roots in pantomime, British drag is captivating, fun and all-round camp."

TRUE NORTH STRONG AND FIERCE

Courtney Conquers

Freezing weather never stopped Canadians from … well, anything, really, and drag is no exception. The country's multifaceted drag history mirrors the national identity: patchworked from a mosaic of influences. From coast to coast, over Rockies and prairies, the range of Canadian drag is as large as Canada itself. Canadian drag artists are adaptable. Their style and technique change with trends, politics, even seasons.

PREVIOUS PAGE: Venus is a Red River Métis two-spirit person and winner of season 4 of *Canada's Drag Race*.

BELOW: The Dumbells in their 1917 skit *Big Beauty Chorus*. Marie, or Allan G. Murray, stands in the centre.

During harsh winters, you'll catch them hosting in rhinestoned parkas and ice skates. In summer heat, they pour water over themselves at parking-lot brunches. Donning a wig in sub-zero temperatures or muggy humidity is routine. Performers combine quirky Canadian humour with intelligent edge to twirl in the same extreme conditions in which they live. This is particularly true of Canadian drag kings; if the queens are tenacious, the kings are Braeön!

Canadian drag may look comfortingly familiar, but its scenes are nuanced. Vancouver memorizes not just lyrics but also Land Acknowledgments. Toronto has unmatched stamina from 'marathon drag'. Have you ever seen a pageant in a barn? Visit the prairies! Want to kiss a codfish with a drag queen? Go to Newfoundland!

Julian Eltinge

FROM DUMBELLS TO DIVE BARS TO DRAG RACE

The evolution of Canadian drag wasn't linear. The billing of acts described as 'impersonation' in venues in Quebec and Vancouver can be traced back to the 1920s. Toronto's first queer spaces sprouted in 1951, with Edmonton and Calgary following in 1969. Winnipeg's first 'official gay bar' opened in 1970, and Halifax's in 1971. Before the era of tangible queer space, however, drag was mainstream entertainment.

The first touring drag troupe were also troops on tour. The Dumbells, Canadian First World War soldiers stationed in France, did female impersonation. The shows started small but became popular throughout the ranks as viewers reminisced about the ladies they missed. The glamorous costumes contrasted with the dress of local working girls, grandeur being scarce amid the squalor of war. Impersonation was also a rare (and specifically queer) outlet for closeted individuals to express themselves in homophobic times. The Dumbells toured after the war, selling out a run of twelve weeks on Broadway, and the Prince of Wales (later, briefly, King Edward VIII) even gifted Dumbell Marjorie jewellery.

Vancouver's New Orpheum Theatre opened in 1927. Its vaudeville acts, which regularly featured such impersonators as Julian Eltinge, were considered to be family-friendly shows, akin to British pantomimes. 'Drag' had no name, but 'cross-dressing' was an aspect of vaudeville, like comedy. It wasn't associated with queerness until 'deviance' rhetoric changed the perception of it.

Rufus Rockhead opened Montreal's first Black-owned bar, Paradise, in 1928. Over fifty years Paradise hosted Billie Holiday, Louis Armstrong and Ella Fitzgerald, but also hired 'unique cabaret acts'. When Paradise booked Dick Montgomery, a Black cabaret dancer who billed herself as a 'female impersonator', it was possibly the first advertised drag show to be held in Quebec.

Like the country itself, the acceptance of drag in Canada was influenced by British colonizers and Americanism. Canada wasn't subject to Hollywood's Hays Code of 1934, under which 'immoral' homosexuality was forbidden in film until the code was repealed in 1968, or affected by the British Board of Film Censors' outlawing of the depiction of 'illicit sexual relationships', but even without local consequences Canadian entertainment forbade 'cross-dressing'. Queerphobic cultural shifts discouraged the Dumbells from performing during the Second World War as the top ranks suspected 'deviant homosexual intention'.

In 1948 Canada *did* pass Criminal Code changes that deemed queer people 'criminal sexual psychopaths' and 'dangerous sexual offenders'. The prospect of prison for those even merely suspected of 'homosexual behaviour' drove queer nightlife underground. In 1950s Toronto, the

ABOVE: Julian Eltinge started female impersonation in 1904 and quickly became world renowned. This Vaudeville poster for Eltinge's act is from 1923. Eltinge successfully toured the world, performed for British Royalty, and regularly appeared at Vancouver's New Orpheum Theatre.

lesbian musician Sarah Dunlop carved out space for three gay men to do cabaret dressed as women. She posted trusted lookouts at the door against the Royal Canadian Mounted Police, which had fired all queer officers as part of a purge from the 1950s onwards and created a division for 'outing homosexuals'. One lookout was Russell Alldread – a young Michelle DuBarry (of whom more below).

As Toronto bars instituted the use of passwords, hostility grew in 1950s Vancouver. Anti-queer fearmongering pushed impersonators out of theatres. To avoid being outed, some queers turned on more visible compatriots for being 'risky' to associate with. Nuanced vocabulary was non-existent, so people who were probably transgender faced malice alongside drag performers. Some Canadians dressed 'in drag' through the 1950s, 60s and 70s in direct defiance of police.

In 1958, ted northe advocated in drag on the steps of the Vancouver Courthouse for the decriminalization of homosexuality, holding a sign proclaiming 'I am a human being.' Cold War paranoia painted queer people as susceptible to Communist influence, but northe – who used lower-case letters in keeping with her counterculture nature – organized letter-writing campaigns to urge Members of Parliament to protect 'gay rights' (back then, 'gay' referred to all queers). In 1967 Prime Minister Pierre Elliott Trudeau proposed legislation decriminalizing homosexuality. Bill C-150 was passed in 1969. Trudeau famously quipped, 'There's no place for the state in the bedrooms of the nation.' He telephoned northe, recognizing her as Empress of Canada in the country's Imperial Court System – a prestigious philanthropic drag society with international ties – by addressing her as 'Your Majesty'.

The normalization of queerness in media began. Following the Stonewall riots in New York City in 1969 came Ottawa's 'We Demand' rally in 1972, then Manitoba's abandonment of queer censorship, and Toronto's first local queer docuseries. Quebec outlawed discrimination on grounds of sexual orientation in 1977, following raids on gay bathhouses. Ontario took until 1986, despite Operation Soap of 1981, Canada's largest mass arrest of queer people, an event that motivated Toronto's first Pride parade that same year.

Canadian national television first featured drag in 1979, when queens Mavis and Carmel Ann set up a kissing booth at Quidi Vidi Lake in Halifax during the Royal St John's Regatta for the first show by the Wonderful Grand Band. They didn't sell many kisses, but they made a good-natured stir. WGB became the highest-rated show in 1980s Newfoundland, and both queens featured continually. It showed drag amicably, in public in daylight. Importantly, these were working drag queens, not straight actors.

By the 1980s drag was seeking real stages again. In 1983 Vancouver's Orpheum billed the 'Ms. Alternate Pageant' to the general public, just like vaudeville. Today, the Orpheum hosts such productions as *RuPaul's Drag Race: Werq the World*, the longest-running international drag tour in history.

ORPHEUM THEATRE

CANADA'S 2ND ANNUAL COMPETITION FOR FEMALE IMPERSONATORS

Featuring last year's Mr. Alternate Christopher Peterson, and your favourite M.C., Rusty from "The Great Imposters."

"and this is the social event of the year". Marke Andrews, Vancouver Sun.

THE ALTERNATE Pageant

"All drag is political, but Indigenous, migrant and racialized drag constitute radical acts of survival."

Canada's reputation is multicultural. Representation there is not perfect, but many cultures have an impact on media and policy. The significance of Indigenous peoples is evident in public art and radio programming, among other things. This multicultural influence is equally unmistakable in Canadian drag. The diversity of the scene stems from migrant and Indigenous artists weaving their experience into style and performance.

Despite being Canada's First Nations, Indigenous people have historically not received the same recognition or opportunity as white settlers. For this reason, Canadian drag has involved discourse about reparations within queer spaces. Reconciliation work is normalizing Land Acknowledgments at drag events, whereby the hosts acknowledge that the event takes place on lands originally owned and inhabited by Indigenous peoples. Acknowledgments cater to specific areas, naming tribes, treaties, languages and original names. Best practices evolve, but most effective Acknowledgments call for action and raise awareness of the *current* crises Indigenous people face. Words are not enough; allyship requires follow-up, including hiring Indigenous artists and dismantling racist pay gaps.

For some artists, Indigeneity and queerness intersect in being two-spirit, a specifically Indigenous identity for those with both male and female spirits. Two-spirit falls under the transgender umbrella, but is differentiated by cultural ties. Non-Indigenous people may be bigender, for example, but they lack the heritage to claim two-spirit.

Queer migrants also blend drag and culture through dress and music. Not every new Canadian limits themselves to cultural performance; it might be one facet of their drag, or not feature at all. For many, however, the intersectionality of being not just a queer person and a Canadian drag artist but also from an immigrant family is at the heart of what they create, just as those intrinsic experiences are central to the way they navigate Canadian society.

The art of marginalized performers isn't always intentionally politicized, but such entertainers are representation. For some, drag means the reclamation of space. Canadian entertainers often use stages to call out systemic inequity. *All* drag is political, but Indigenous, migrant and racialized drag constitute radical acts of survival.

OPPOSITE: A flyer for the 1983 'Ms. Alternate Pageant', the first drag show to be featured on the Orpheum stage in Vancouver since 'cross-dressing' was criminalized out of the Vaudeville circuit in the 1940s. The show was emceed by Rusty Ryan, famed member of the touring Canadian drag troupe The Great Imposters, which she started in 1972. Michelle DuBarry was also a member of the Imposters.

SPILLING THE TEA: CANADIAN DRAG FOLKLORE

Drag artists love a story, which is good because until recently, drag nuances were mostly preserved orally. Facts weren't always documented (sometimes intentionally) in high-risk eras. That's why drag folklore is important. Even with embellishment, retelling tales uncovers drag history that might otherwise be lost.

Canadian drag folklore dates back to the nineteenth century – sort of! The Albion Hotel opened in Guelph in 1867 and was the second Ontario establishment to obtain a liquor licence. Its house brew attracted the American gangster Al Capone and, allegedly, one of his mistresses was murdered there. More contemporarily, the Albion's lounge became home to Drag Trivia nights when local performers were still searching for willing venues. The building stands partially empty now, but how appropriately camp that a (potentially haunted) historical site was among the first of the Guelph businesses to open its doors to modern drag!

Café Cléopâtre in Montreal has welcomed sex workers since 1976: many of them trans, all cash-tipped. As drag queens built careers, transphobia discouraged them from following suit. Queens demanded alcohol to avoid comparison with these contentious colleagues, quipping, 'You paid at the door. Get me a shot instead.' This delayed tipping in Quebec (see page 200).

Before filming the 1978 movie *La Cage aux Folles* (on which *The Birdcage* of 1996 was based), its producers visited Montreal to research drag. In 1970s Quebec, entertainers were required by law to reveal their identity at the end of each show. The producers learned this at curtain call, when queens removed their wigs to avoid charges of 'tricking' the audience.

In Alberta's police raids of the 1980s, those wearing fewer than two articles of clothing appropriate for their assigned gender were arrested. Undergarments could be hidden, but still help the wearer to avoid charges of 'illegal crossdressing'. That's why the Edmonton legend Twiggy still wears men's underwear and socks in drag. Laws change, but old habits die hard.

Did you know *RuPaul's Drag Race* wasn't the first competition to bear that name? Edmonton's gay club Flashback hosted 'drag races' during its pageants of the 1980s and 90s. Drunk regulars raced one another – in drag – through an alleyway of dunk tanks, wet T-shirt contests and Jell-O wrestling. Mado Lamotte, owner of Cabaret Mado in Montreal, also hosts a competition called Drag Race that pre-dates RuPaul's. It began in 2000 and still takes place annually at the St-Ambroise Montreal Fringe Festival.

WELCOME TO THE SHOWS

A country this large can't help but have range. The drag in one province isn't standard everywhere; etiquette, structure, venues and lingo fluctuate. Some elements persist nationwide, while others surprise even fellow Canadians. Queer bars are still home base, but Canadian drag happens anywhere. Television put it on the world stage … and in restaurants, town squares, farms, beaches, railway stations and funerals. Even the Calgary Stampede (a famous Albertan rodeo) features drag now.

When it comes to lingo, Quebec varies. Most hosting is in French; English inclusion depends on location. Smaller shows used to francophone audiences don't always cater to anglophones. In such cities as Montreal,

OPPOSITE: Vancouver drag queen The Girlfriend Experience stuns at *DragCon UK* shortly after appearing on *Canada's Drag Race* Season 4. Before appearing on the show, Girlfriend, a trans woman, noticed a deficit of trans-lead information as she sought gender affirming healthcare. She gained notoriety for using social media to document her own experiences from consultation through to recovery in vulnerable detail to help educate other trans people seeking the advice she hadn't been able to find herself.

however, hosts spot confused tourists quickly. They'll tease you, but they'll switch language occasionally. In either language, francophones often say 'drags' instead of 'king' or 'queen', which amuses those from other provinces.

Toronto's quirk is 'marathon drag'. The city does have other shows, but marathon reigns. Two or three artists (who might do early shows at one bar, and late shows next door) alternate for sets of three back-to-back numbers, a minute on the mic, then a couple more songs, rotating until the finale duets. Toronto performers regularly do sixteen numbers per show.

Elsewhere, numbers vary as widely as the crowds. Lip-syncing persists, but artists also do impersonation, comedy, singing, dancing, acrobatics and circus tricks. Drag still brings queer adults to nightlife, but its unprecedented acceptance has adapted it for straight crowds, children, professionals, students and older people. Although queer spaces maintain sanctity and grit, Canadian artists frequently perform for the mainstream.

EX-PATS, ICONS AND TRANS-CANADA EXCELLENCE

Learning queer history is pivotal to engaging authentically with drag. Drag icons and milestones are no longer relegated to hearsay and oral tradition; the contemporary era is better preserved. This has enriched drag so that it's more educational and more referential than ever. It also teaches us to value living legends as they pave the way, not just after they've passed. Canada's litany of leaders, past and present, defies expectations, binaries and borders.

Have you heard of the Trans-Canada Highway? Like drivers, drag fans should heed the prefix 'trans-'. Canadian drag performers owe most of their current opportunities to the transgender entertainers who graced stages before them. Trans icons of auld didn't have today's lexicon; some 'impersonators' rarely removed their persona, conflating performance and daily presentation. Their stories are woven into narratives that don't mention transness. Perhaps that's why contemporary trans Canadians are intentionally out and proud as they perform, produce and teach.

Even in the 1960s, however, Montreal's Lana St-Cyr *did* publicly claim a 'trans' identity (although she employed the term 'transsexual' as opposed to the contemporary word 'transgender', as the former was more popular at the time). Lana performed drag burlesque with live snakes, and took onstage bubble baths. In 1962 she was arrested for 'indecency' and escorted out of Café Beaver. *Le Nouveau Journal* published her photo, granting her infamy by querying whether the judge should call her 'Miss' or 'Sir'. The arrest was part of Montreal's crackdown on 'deceptive clubs' – drag shows – in advance of Expo 67, a World's Fair celebrating Canada's centennial. Lana later wowed celebrities with her bubbles at Club 82 in New York.

Clearly, Canadian drag going international pre-dates *Drag Race* – especially through pageantry. The country's most famous drag export is Brooke Lynn Hytes, the first Canadian cast member on *RuPaul's Drag Race*.

OPPOSITE: Queen of the North, Brooke Lynn Hytes is a trained ballerina and host of *Canada's Drag Race*. Before becoming a career drag queen, she toured as a dancer with the drag ballet, *Les Ballets Trockadero de Monte Carlo*. Hytes is also the one queen in *One Queen, Five Queers*, a Canadian TV show based on the 2009 cultural phenomenon, *One Girl, Five Gays*.

Brooke Lynn gained notoriety as 'Miss Continental' 2014, the second Canadian winner following Tulsi in 2008. She was hired at the American showbar Play Nashville, cementing a green card, and after *RuPaul's Drag Race*, she became the host of *Canada's Drag Race*, the third spin-off behind Thailand (see page 69) and the UK (see page 159). In contrast, such performers as Tynomi Banks and Miss Conception maintain Canadian addresses despite entertaining cross-border.

Not everyone with global impact travels. Besides a lengthy career, pageant titles and Imperial Court of Toronto philanthropy, two-time Empress Michelle DuBarry is the oldest drag queen in the world. She was awarded the Guinness World Record for Oldest Performing Drag Queen in 2015, at eighty-four. Dispute arose as the American legend Darcelle XV was one year older. The record was transferred in 2016 and Darcelle held it until her passing in 2023, when Michelle, then ninety-one, was re-crowned.

OH, CANADA!

Canada and its drag are anything but monolithic. The scene is classic but diverse, recognizable but unique. This cocktail of quirky humour, adaptability, good manners, strong work ethic and variegated influence charms the world and sets Canada and Canadians apart. 'Fierce' applies to the quality of the country's drag, but also to its fortitude.

ABOVE: Now in her 90s, Toronto legend Michelle DuBarry still goes out in drag to tip younger queens or raise money for charity. She guested on an episode of *Canada's Drag Race* Season 1 in 2020.

OPPOSITE: Prince Manny Dingo performs in Toronto in 2021. Dingo's drag is known for creative outfits, colourful makeup and hair, and high-energy, almost acrobatic, dancing. He often performs his own popular recorded track, 'Take It'.

REBELLION AND RESISTANCE

Alex Nolos

Come early September in Bushwick, New York, the heat isn't quite unbearable, but it's certainly uncomfortable. So, when one walks up the gravel yard into the Knockdown Center for Bushwig, it's easy to understand the guts it takes to face the crowds under a wig, greasepaint, lashes, latex, tulle, synthetic fabrics of all textures, Pleaser shoes, pads and/or rigorously engineered mechanical costumes that turn a human into a beast of the queer imagination.

The Bushwig drag and music festival draws performers and attendees from all corners of the globe for a two-day extravaganza, which casts a spotlight over a broad spectrum of artists: performers from the local drag community, iconic drag artists, representatives of the legendary ballroom houses, RuGirls … and the famed whistle-blower Chelsea Manning. Such is the American drag ecosystem.

Bushwig's roster extends past the mainland United States, inviting performers from around the world, as befits a population descended from centuries of colonialism, resilience and resistance. On our tour of American drag, it is important that we be mindful of the United States' position in the world as a massive colonizing force. As performers and audiences, we must be aware of our place in this framework and work to change our ways of thinking and living in order to support the artistry of drag performers who fight this colonization every day.

WHAT TO EXPECT WHEN YOU'RE SERVING

The modern American drag landscape is too massive to categorize easily, but the more liberal metropolitan centres, such as New York City, tend to draw in drag excellence from across the country, especially as a political backlash against trans people and drag has mounted elsewhere over the last

few years. Drag shows in New York can take many forms, and Brooklyn in particular is known for supporting a wide variety of drag that crosses over into other art forms, such as theatre, music, photography and film. New York's drag population is well known for its inclusivity and ingenuity, and has supported the careers of such well-known contemporary artists as Sasha Velour, Murray Hill and Candis Cayne.

New York is, of course, not the only drag scene in the United States, and it would be remiss not to acknowledge the vibrancy of drag scenes elsewhere in the country. It is especially important to give credit to performers who are working in states where drag is being targeted by lawmakers amid the backlash against LGBTQ+ rights.

Historically, metropolitan hubs across the States have become known for certain styles of drag. Texas is synonymous with drag pageantry, lavish competitions packed with floor-length dresses, high-femme glamour and towering wigs that nod to the old adage that everything is bigger in Texas. Chicago's ever-expanding drag scene is famous for its diversity and DIY spirit, whereas Atlanta is increasingly known for its drag-king scene (Manhole, the city's first regular night made up entirely of drag kings, was established in 2021 and continues to go from strength to strength).

Regardless of location, the greatest divide among performers exists between 'mainstream' and 'alternative' drag. The line separating these definitions is blurry, but there can be a little or a lot of animosity between performers from different scenes, especially since mainstream-style drag tends to correspond with drag that excludes non-queen, non-cisgender

and non-white performers. However, there can also be overlap and camaraderie between scenes, with alternative performers crossing over to perform in mainstream venues and vice versa. For example, the performers La Zavaleta, ShowPonii and West Dakota practise versatility by performing drag of all kinds, from high-pageant glam to oddball to downright nasty punk, in venues of all types.

Alternative drag is especially popular in San Francisco, Chicago and Brooklyn, among other places, but it is important to note that not all performers align with the term 'alternative', which is used here as shorthand for drag that is experimental, boundary-less and inclusive of kings, things, trans performers and non-white performers. It's a wide spectrum: there are 'drag terrorists', such as the gleefully grotesque performance artist Christeene; deliciously dark drag queens like Maddelynn Hatter; and groundbreaking drag artists like DeFacto Obsolete, whose electrifying performances often include live acts of body modification.

A popular way to foster emerging drag styles and artists is through competitions. For instance, La Zavaleta's Bitchfest, a competition that began pre-COVID-19 and re-emerged in 2022, has reinvigorated the work of existing performers and kick-started the careers of new drag artists in Brooklyn. Contestants have included such queens as Miss Ma'amShe and Dawn; drag things, such as Jay Kay and the currently reigning Maxx

ABOVE: From left: Paris Alexander, La Zavaleta, and Groovy Bluez after a round of Bitchfest in 2023.

> "In ballroom, houses serve several purposes. They are art collectives, performance groups, dance teams and, most importantly, families."

Love; and kings, among them ShowPonii and TJ Maxxx. There is also the Takes the Cake competition hosted by the Cake Boys, a drag-king collective comprised of Muscles Monty, Richard, Senerio and Sweaty Eddie, which is centred on kings and things as a way to highlight non-queen drag.

THE FIRST AMERICAN DRAG QUEEN AND HER LEGACY

Drag has always existed as a performance art that acts against whatever dominating force may be in power against queer people at the time. The first American performer we know to have identified as a 'queen of drag' is one William Dorsey Swann. Swann was born enslaved in 1860, just before the Civil War, after which his parents were released from slavery. One account of Swann's early adulthood tells of how, at the age of twenty-two, he was given jail time for a charge of petty larceny; he had stolen books and an unnamed item from his employer. Remarkably, his employer filed for a presidential pardon on Swann's behalf, since 'he was free from vice, industrious, refined in his habits and associations, gentle in his disposition, [and] courteous in his bearing,' and he noted that the items were stolen in an effort to improve Swann's education.

We do not know if the pardon was granted, but we do know that, further into his adulthood, Swann made history by becoming the first American to exercise their legal rights in defence of queer people. In the 1880s and 90s he began hosting drag balls. Because homosexuality and cross-dressing were illegal, these were held in secret, but on 1 January 1896 one of them was raided, resulting in charges being brought against Swann for 'running a disorderly house' (a common euphemism for running a brothel). While there is a significant overlap between sex work and drag (as is common for marginalized communities that may rely on sex work for survival), we do not know if the former was actually taking place at the balls, and at the time it would have been very possible for such a charge to be levelled against a gathering of queer people based solely on discrimination and stigma against sex work. Swann was sentenced to 300 days in jail, and shortly after beginning his sentence, he filed an appeal, this time on his own behalf. The appeal was signed by thirty of his supporters, probably members of the queer community. Although the appeal was not successful, it made history as the first legal action attempting to protect the queer community's right to gather, preceding the Compton's Cafeteria and Stonewall riots by some time. After finishing his sentence Swann continued to host balls; he died in 1925.

These balls were an early predecessor of modern drag balls, such as those of the Harlem ball scene. Some accounts even indicate that a popular dance of the time, the cakewalk, may be an ancestor of voguing. Ballroom and drag are distinct art forms, but they have a heavy influence on each other, and many performers exist in both scenes. Ball culture was revived in the 1960s as a re-invention of the Black and Latinx community of New York City. You might be familiar with the line: 'Look at her make-up! It's *terrible*!' This quotation comes from the luminescent Crystal LaBeija, featured in *The Queen* (1968), a documentary film about a drag pageant hosted by Flawless Sabrina. This iconic line is more than just a read, however. It's a criticism of the favour shown to white contestants in drag pageants of the time. Crystal – a Black queen who lost the pageant to a white queen of lesser talent – reacted by becoming the first mother of the House of LaBeija, reviving the ball scene that had lain dormant since Swann's heyday.

In ballroom, houses serve several purposes. They are art collectives, performance groups, dance teams and, most importantly, families. Ball culture was an antidote not only to the racism *within* the queer community, but also to the need many gay and trans people had – and still have – for families, having often been disowned by their blood relatives. Voguing is perhaps ball culture's best-known export, given its appropriation by Madonna for her single 'Vogue' in 1990. As drag has come into the mainstream, ball culture has gained new appreciation and

interest through such queens as Aja and Olivia Lux, who are known for their work in ballroom. Aja in particular has used her platform to be a fierce defender of ballroom culture and its preservation in drag, working to correct the misappropriation of ballroom vocabulary and aesthetics. Voguing remains a compelling art form, with its sharp moves and acrobatics drawing newcomers into the love of the ball.

Y'ALL BETTER QUIET DOWN: STONEWALL AND SYLVIA

It is impossible to think about American drag without thinking of the most famous act of queer resistance on the books: the Stonewall riots of 1969. Optimistically, one might think the queer community in the USA has always welcomed drag, but both past and present times have shown this to be complicated. Take, for example, the words of the icon and activist Sylvia Rivera about the Stonewall itself:

> What people fail to realize is that the Stonewall was not a drag queen bar. It was a white male bar for middle-class males to pick up young boys of different races. Very few drag queens were allowed in there, because if they had allowed drag queens into the club, it would have brought the club down.

ABOVE: Sylvia Rivera marching with STAR (Street Transvestite Action Revolutionaries).

Rivera goes on to explain:

> *The main drag queen bar at that time was the Washington Square Bar on Third Street and Broadway. That's where you found diesel dykes and drag queens and their lovers. Oh, yeah, we mixed with lesbians. We always got along together back then. All that division between the lesbian women and queens came after 1974 when Jean O'Leary and the radical lesbians came up. The radicals did not accept us or masculine-looking women who dressed like men. And those lesbian women might not even have been trans. But we did get along famously in the early 60s. I've been to many a dyke party. And transgendered men back then were living and working. I met many who were working and living as men with their female lovers. They were highly respected.*

Queer solidarity across different sectors of the community – such as drag queens, trans women, lesbians and trans men, as Rivera describes – is a key element of the survival of drag, and a testament to the way these communities overlap. For example, a single individual could be a

ABOVE: Olivia Lux performs during *RuPaul's DragCon LA*, in May 2023.

> "Queer solidarity across different sectors of the community is a key element of the survival of drag, and a testament to the way these communities overlap."

transmasc lesbian drag queen, and spaces where all in the community are welcome are crucial for the vibrancy and freedom that drag fosters. When it comes to Stonewall, we have a complicated story of an event that marked a massive shift in queer history, but the fallout reveals biases and discrimination within the community, not just outside it.

For those who are unfamiliar with the events at Stonewall, here they are in a nutshell. What began as an ordinary night – and an ordinary police raid – at the Stonewall gay bar on 28 June 1969 turned into a massive riot when, unlike during previous raids, the patrons resisted the police. They did so to the degree that the disturbance lasted for days, drawing unheard-of press attention and sending a clear message that the gay community had had it with the status quo. Thus was born the modern gay rights movement and the recognition of June as Gay Pride month. The first Pride marches took place just a year after the uprising. There is much more to Stonewall as an event, but what is especially relevant to the drag community is that while drag queens, trans people and people of colour were on the front lines of the action that night and in resistances in general, they were largely left behind by the civil rights progress that followed the riot.

As Rivera described, drag queens (note that many self-identified drag queens of the time used the term in tandem and sometimes synonymously with what we would now consider trans identity; here I use the language they used for themselves) and other gender anarchists suffered the brunt of the violence of Stonewall and the period as a whole, yet were met with distaste and disrespect by queer people with more privilege and 'respectability'. In her famous 'Y'all better quiet down' speech from the Christopher Street Liberation Day Rally in 1973, Rivera said:

> *You all tell me, go and hide my tail between my legs. I will no longer put up with this shit. I have been beaten, I have had my nose broken, I have been thrown in jail, I have lost my job, I have lost my apartment, for gay liberation, and you all treat me this way?*

RISING RENT, RESILIENCE AND RESISTANCE

The history of American drag is ultimately one of resistance, and queer performers and venues alike are accustomed to adversity. Whether it's against zoning laws, local hostility or the Mafia, queer spaces and their patrons have perfected the art of resilience. San Francisco, one of the gay capitals of the world, site of the Compton's Cafeteria riots of 1966 (pre-dating Stonewall), host of the annual Folsom Street Fair and birthplace of the charitable protest movement the Sisters of Perpetual Indulgence, was once home to the Stud, a queer leather bar in the South of Market (SoMa) neighbourhood. The Stud was a landmark, beginning

as a primarily gay male space but over time becoming a countercultural bar for all queer people. In the late 1970s it was even a frequent gathering spot for Harvey Milk (the first openly gay elected official in California) and his team. The Stud's existence faced a serious threat in 2016, when rising rent and the owner's retirement brought the possibility of closure. The local community banded together to keep the bar open, and it was bought by a collective of nightlife professionals including the activist, politician and drag queen Honey Mahogany. Despite the efforts of the community, gentrification and ever-increasing rent meant that the bar was unable to reopen, but the Stud hasn't disappeared. It continues to operate, after a fashion, as a roaming collective that puts on shows in a variety of spaces, again supported by the community it has fostered since 1966.

The story of the Stud symbolizes American histories of queer struggle and resistance, which have always been tied up with drag. Just as Honey Mahogany stepped up to save the Stud, drag artists – such as Stormé DeLarverie, a Black drag king who played a pivotal role in the Stonewall riots – have long been instrumental in keeping queer culture alive.

San Francisco is also the birthplace of a current target of conservative backlash: Drag Queen Story Hour. DQSH was not, in fact, started by drag queens, but rather by the author and organizer Michelle Tea. After bringing her child to book-readings at the public library and finding them

ABOVE: The Sisters of Perpetual Indulgence at a West Hollywood Pride march, 2016.

insufficiently inclusive of queer families, Tea came up with the idea of queer-centred reading led by drag queens at public libraries, free to attend, and offering families an opportunity to discuss gender identity and queerness with their children. Radar Productions, a non-profit literary organization based in San Francisco, put on the first events in 2015, and – being a simple concept that is easy to execute – it was not long before DQSH spread. There are now DQSH chapters not only in the USA, but also in Europe, Asia and Australia (see page 18).

The current moral panic against queer people in the United States has found an effective tactic in building a conspiracy that such people are trying to indoctrinate children into their 'ideology' by convincing them to join their number. Many of those who uphold these beliefs believe that queerness is a choice people make or an illness that one can be infected with. Insidiously, however, others believe that there are many queer people who are genuine, but that there is a sinister cabal of queers whose goal is to take straight, cis children and 'turn' them. This latter view is typically used to allow white cis queers to be accepted and assimilate easily into mainstream life, while continuing to enact violence against Black, brown, trans and other queer people who do not have the option to assimilate. This is what Rivera fought against: the neglect of 'difficult' queers by members of the community who are able to remake themselves in the image of straights. Sadly, there are many gay people who protest such initiatives as Drag Queen Story Hour, and it is no coincidence that those people are often white, cis or 'passing'.

SHOWS

Coming back to where we started, Bushwig's annual festivities allow the many unique and wonderful styles of American drag to come together in an event that is part showcase, part family reunion. Whether feast or famine, these chances to connect are crucial for the queer community, and such events are a beautiful example of the way that drag creates these spaces not only for performers, but also for anyone who needs them.

ALL EYES ON THE CARNIVAL

Juliana Santos

Many people outside Brazil who think or hear about this wonderful country know only Rio de Janeiro and São Paulo as cities, and soccer and Carnival as entertainment. But Brazil is much more than that. It's important to understand how big it is, with its twenty-six states (distributed over five regions: North, North-east, Central-West, South-east and South) and one federal district (Brasília). Each state, and even each town and city, has its own culture.

That's why Brazil's artistic sector is so diverse, and that applies to the art of drag as well. The history of Brazilian drag is wide-ranging, but much of the available information refers to the South-east (the states of Espírito Santo, Minas Gerais, São Paulo and Rio de Janeiro) and the South (Paraná, Santa Catarina and Rio Grande do Sul). São Paulo stands out, because it is one of the country's greatest cities in terms not only of population but also of cultural diversity, resembling other world metropolises such as New York, Tokyo, Shanghai and Buenos Aires.

THE FIRST SIGNS OF DRAG

The precursors of the art of drag in Brazil appeared in the 1960s and 70s, and were called 'cross-dressers' (*transformistas*). The name was given to artists who performed in swimsuits and dresses while dancing, singing or acting.

The first drag queen in Brazil was Madame Satã, João Francisco dos Santos. He was born in the northern state of Pernambuco in 1900 and had a very hard childhood, moving to Rio in 1907, when his mother exchanged him for a horse in order to support his seventeen siblings. When he was twenty-two, the French revue company Ba-ta-clan came to Rio, and from that moment dos Santos knew he wanted to be an artiste. He made his debut as a drag queen in 1928 at the Casa de Caboclo theatre, where he played Mulata do Balacochê in *Loucos em Copacabana (Crazy in Copacabana)*.

In 1938 dos Santos won a carnival costume contest dressed as a sequined bat, inspired by a distinctive bat from his home state. A few days later, however, he was arrested with a group of 'transvestites' for being gay, and was recognized by the chief of police as the winner of the contest. (In Brazil, *travestis*, 'transvestites', were men who dressed up as women to sell sex, which was illegal at the time. There were also trans people and, since the word 'trans' wasn't used yet, they were known as transvestites.) The chief immediately associated the bat costume with the film *Madam Satan* (1930), directed by Cecil B. DeMille, and gave dos Santos the nickname Madame Satã. In the beginning, dos Santos didn't like it much, but he held on to it for the rest of this life. In 1950 he started impersonating the celebrated singer and actor Carmen Miranda in a new theatre in Rio. The act was a great success and expanded to become a show in a nightclub called Cafona's. At seventy-four years old, dos Santos was still working in a musical called *Lampião no Inferno*, in which he played the devil. He died of pulmonary cancer at the age of seventy-six.

PREVIOUS PAGE: Lorelay Fox, pioneer of drag queens on YouTube, with over one million subscribers.

OPPOSITE: Madame Satã became Brazil's first drag queen in 1928.

THE LONGEST CAREER UNDER A WIG

Eduardo Albarella, known as Miss Biá, was another very early 'cross-dresser' or drag queen in Brazil. Miss Biá began cross-dressing in São Paulo in about 1960, at the age of twenty-one. Lip-syncing as we now know it was not common at that time, so the only option was live singing. There were also no LGBTQ+ clubs, so the drag queens performed in straight clubs and bars – which were packed, since everyone was curious to see something new and different. The military dictatorship that began in Brazil in 1964 prohibited men from dressing up as women, so Miss Biá had to perform as a man until the law was revoked (as part of the process of 'Abertura Política' (Political Opening) during which most of the laws created during the dictatorship between 1974 and 1988 were revoked) and

she could perform as a drag queen once again. It wasn't easy to be a cross-dresser during that era, even after the law changed. A drag queen on her way to a venue had to carry her wig, since if she were caught wearing it she would be arrested as an illegal sex worker. Miss Biá performed at many venues in São Paulo, including La Vie en Rose, Nostro Mondo, Medieval and Corintho. In 2018 she performed at *Priscilla*, a drag festival famous for having RuGirls as its main guests. Miss Biá's career in drag lasted for fifty-nine years, and she died in 2020 at the age of eighty-one.

SAFE SPACES

The first gay club with drag shows in São Paulo was called Nostro Mondo. Owned by the lawyer and probation officer Clóvis Vieira, also known as Condessa Mônica, it opened on the night of 30 April 1971, in the middle of the military dictatorship. Vieira was inspired by the Stonewall riots in New York City in 1969 to open a safe space for the LGBTQ+ community in Brazil. One of the segments of the show presented at his club was *Condessa Invites*, effectively a precursor of today's chat shows. Vieira came out as trans in the 1980s, and underwent gender reassignment surgery in May 1989, sadly passing away the following month. Nostro Mondo, which became the oldest continuously open LGBTQ+ entertainment establishment in São Paulo and perhaps even the whole of Brazil, finally closed its doors in 2014, after forty-three years.

Nevertheless, some of the drag queens who are active on the scene today started out at Nostro Mondo. Márcia Pantera, for example, was a pioneer of *bate-cabelo* (a dance style inspired by rockers – also known as headbangers – who used to toss their heads and long hair to the sound of the guitars) in Brazil. Another queen who graced the stage of Nostro Mondo, and indeed who graces stages all over Brazil these days, is Silvetty Montilla. She is best known for being a stand-up comedian and hostess, but also has experience as an actor, performer and singer. On 28 June 1997 she made a speech at the first São Paulo Pride parade.

The next club to open its doors and hold shows was Medieval, which opened on 19 August 1971, also in São Paulo. The shows held there were inspired by Broadway and the Parisian cabarets, with all their attendant glamour, and attracted people of all kinds, celebrities included. Every year the club held a themed anniversary party called Broadway Night. It was a hotly anticipated evening, and people would line the streets to see the guests arriving in their extravagant costumes. In 1976, for example, the actor Wilza Carla dressed as an odalisque and arrived at the club riding an elephant. Another great entrance was made by the promoter Darby Daniel, who came dressed as Snow White inside a glass coffin carried by seven dwarves; his prince, on a white horse, waited for him at the door of the club.

ABOVE: Condessa Mônica, who owned Nostro Mondo, the first gay club with drag shows in São Paulo.

OPPOSITE: Márcia Pantera, who started out at Nostro Mondo.

DRAG AS POLITICAL ACT

The theatre group Dzi Croquettes, which started on 8 August 1972 during the most repressive period of the military regime, was made up of thirteen gay men and criticized political institutions with humour. The group also displayed all kinds of sexuality, from androgyny to the most feminine. Their performance was not just a great show, it was also a political act, intended to bring down prejudice of all kinds. The inspiration came from cabaret and the Rio Carnival, which was the only legitimate opportunity at that time for men to dress up as women. During the four years of its existence, Dzi Croquettes was forced to close for more than a month under the laws of the dictatorship, until an agreement was reached to allow it to continue. The group also took their show to Paris, where it was at first boycotted by the press, until Liza Minnelli (who thought of herself as the group's godmother) brought guests to watch it. Despite its short life, Dzi Croquettes inspired many contemporary drag performers and other artists across Brazil.

ABOVE: Brazilian drag queen and singer Pabllo Vittar performs onstage during the NOS Primavera Sound in Portugal in June 2022.

QUEENS FOR THE CAUSE

Another important figure in early Brazilian drag history is the model, actor and host Elke Maravilha. Born in Germany in 1945, she moved to Brazil as a child and made the country her home. She was known for her extravagant dressing and exuberant wigs, and for her advocacy of the LGBTQ+ community. The first guest on her talk show *Programa Elke Maravilha* was Jorge Lafond, a Rio-born dancer, actor and comedian who featured on several television shows until he landed his most iconic role, the drag queen Vera Verão. Vera had her own segment in a comedy show called *A Praça é Nossa* (*Our Place*), and a catchphrase that is still well known: 'Êêêêpa! Bicha não!' (something like 'Yeah! Fag, my ass!'). During Lafond's interview with Maravilha, they discussed the difficulties he faced from being Black and homosexual. Maravilha also performed a gay

ABOVE: Ikaro Kadoshi, Penelopy Jean
and Rita von Hunty, hosts of the show
Drag Me as a Queen.

wedding on live television (not a real one, since same-sex weddings were
not legal or valid at the time). The subjects Maravilha covered were so
controversial that her show lasted for only four months, despite boosting
its channel's ratings. though she continued as a guest judge on other shows
on the same channel for many years. Even though Maravilha never called
herself a drag queen, many members of the queer community considered
her to be one.

Today, one of the best-known drag queens to come from São Paulo is
Ikaro Kadoshi, who started out in the year 2000. She made history as the
first drag queen from Latin America to host a television show: *Drag Me as
a Queen* (2017–2022) alongside Penelopy Jean and Rita von Hunty. The
reality show ran for two seasons, and reruns are still being shown. Ikaro

was also the first drag queen to enter into a partnership with Nike, becoming the brand's ambassador for LGBTQ+ causes in sports. In 2023 she was one of the hosts for the reality show *Caravana das Drags* (*Queens on the Run*) on Amazon Prime, in which a bus drove around Brazil to meet the ten contestants fighting for the title of *Drag Soberana* (*Queen Supreme*) and a cash prize. Ikaro is known for her mesmerizing performances, overflowing with passion and fire – attributes all Brazilian queens share.

BEGINNINGS IN THE SOUTH

The first gay club to open in Porto Alegre was Flower's, on 8 May 1971, founded by the journalist Dirnei Messias and his friend Elaine Ledur. For the first four years the club employed a cast of eighteen dancers who put on shows inspired by Broadway and by Hollywood movies, such as *Cabaret* and *Sampson and Delilah*. It was the first safe space for drag queens in the city. In 1975, after constant problems with the police, Messias decided to move the club to another spot and renamed it New Flower's City, which lasted another four years.

In the 1980s Gloria Crystal was born, the first *transformista* of the state of Rio Grande do Sul. She used to go to a club called L'Entourage, and one night a producer noticed her there, dancing and lip-syncing with friends. Telling her that she reminded him of an actor friend of his, named Gloria Cristal, he invited her to do a show inspired by his friend, and that's how everything started. Gloria is now very active in politics. A friend of hers, Rebecca McDonald, also became a reference for future *transformistas*. She made her debut on the big screen in 1991 in the short film *Au Revoir Shirlei*, which won the Guarnicê Film Festival award for best cinematography, and she was the first *transformista* to be featured on the cover of a magazine.

Charlene Voluntaire, born Charles Machado, is another of the original Brazilian *transformistas*. As a teenager, Machado was fascinated by and curious about the world of *transformistas* as he saw it on television and in Carnival parades. Later, he went to a gay nightclub called Pantheon, where he saw Rebecca McDonald on stage, and something in him changed. Charlene herself was born years later, in 1994, when Machado accepted an invitation from friends to join their drag-style group House of Dolls. They suggested that he adopt the name Charlene Voluntária ('volunteer'), since he is a very generous person, but he said no, that Charlene needed some glamour in her name, and that's how the French-sounding name Voluntaire came about. Charlene has now been on the scene for decades, always bringing a classic Hollywood touch to her performances.

A *gaúcha* drag queen (a slang term for people from Rio Grande do Sul) inspired by all those mentioned above is Cassandra Calabouço. She made her debut in 1998 in a bar called Ocidente in Porto Alegre, for a friend's

"Brazilian drag queens are among the fiercest queens in the world, and deserve our support."

party, after which she performed twice a week in a club named Século XV – and has never stopped. She created the project 'Pimp My Drag' to help those who want to start doing drag, or for those who already do it and wish to improve their craft and exchange experiences. After twenty-five years on the scene, Cassandra considers herself to be a fun and polished queen who is always ready to set the stage on fire – metaphorically – with her amazing dancing to the sound of Brazilian funk and the songs of Brazilian divas.

GLITTER EVERYWHERE

It is important to keep in mind that, even though progress is made every day, Brazil is still one of the most dangerous countries in which to be a drag queen or part of the LGBTQ+ community. Brazilian drag queens are among the fiercest queens in the world, and deserve our support. They perform with such passion that you can feel it radiating from them, even just for a simple ballad. After all, as the host of *Drag Race Brazil*, Grag Queen, puts it, 'the Brazilian drag queen never gives up'.

OPPOSITE: Cassandra Calabouço, creator of the 'Pimp My Drag' project.

INTRODUCTION

Channing, Gerard Joseph, 'The First Drag Queen Was a Former Slave', The Nation, 31 January 2020, www.thenation.com/article/society/drag-queen-slave-ball.

Dick, M.B. '618–907 AD Tang Dynasty', Drag King History, www.dragkinghistory.com/618-907-a-d-tang-dynasty (accessed 4 April 2024).

AUSTRALIA

Beazley, Jordyn and Sharp-Wiggins, Blake, 'Behind the Scenes at the Miss First Nation Drag Competition: A Photo Essay', The Guardian, 1 March 2023, www.theguardian.com/stage/2023/mar/01/behind-the-scenes-at-the-miss-first-nation-drag-competition-a-photo-essay

Brook, Benedict 'NSW Government Apologises for Ill Treatment of Protesters at Sydney's First Mardi Gras in 1978', News.com.au, 26 February 2016, www.news.com.au/lifestyle/gay-marriage/nsw-government-apologises-for-ill-treatment-of-protesters-at-sydneys-first-mardi-gras-in-1978/news-story/f97a7d6da638968bd9551e0bac3403e5

Buckmaster, Luke 'The Adventures of Priscilla: Five Things You Didn't Know about the Aussie Hit', The Guardian, 17 June 2015, www.theguardian.com/culture/2015/jun/17/the-adventures-of-priscilla-five-things-you-didnt-know

Carmen, Lo, 'Acid, Blood and Police Raids: The Pioneering Drag Chaos of Sylvia and the Synthetics', The Guardian, 25 February 2021, www.theguardian.com/culture/2021/feb/26/acid-blood-and-police-raids-the-pioneering-drag-chaos-of-sylvia-and-the-synthetics

Croome, Rodney, 'Gay Law Reform', 2006, www.utas.edu.au/library/companion_to_tasmanian_history/G/Gay%20Law%20Reform.htm

Del Castillo, Ronald, 'Preserving Priscilla: A History of Gay Identity and the Drag Subculture in Sydney', Ideas in History IV/1 (2012), https://epress.lib.uts.edu.au/student-journals/index.php/iih/article/view/1367

DIVA Awards: www.divaawards.com.au/about.html

Heanue, Siobhan, 'Glitter Never Ages: Film History Preserved in Priscilla Costumes', ABC News, www.abc.net.au/news/2014-02-28/glitter-never-ages-film-history-preserved-in-priscilla-costumes/5291706

Seligman, Craig, 'Yes, Sydney, Australia in the 1960s Was the Drag Capital of the World', LitHub, 3 March 2023, www.lithub.com/yes-sydney-australia-in-the-1960s-was-the-drag-capital-of-the-world

Sydney Mardi Gras: www.mardigras.org.au/history-of-sydney-mardi-gras

We'd also like to acknowledge Anita Wigl'it for her valuable insights for this chapter.

NEW ZEALAND

Aunty Tamara haka: www.tiktok.com/@auntytamaraaa/video/7204963275996466434 (accessed 28 February 2024)

Brickell, Chris, Mates and Lovers: A History of Gay New Zealand, Godwit Press, 2008.

Ibid, 'Drag in 1970s New Zealand', Museum of New Zealand, www.tepapa.govt.nz/discover-collections/read-watch-play/lgbtqi-histories-aotearoa-new-zealand/drag-1970s-new-zealand (accessed 28 February 2024)

'Bucking the Trend: Q&A with Edward Cowley', Cityscape, 14 April 2022, www.cityscape-christchurch.co.nz/blog/people/entry/bucking-the-trend-q-a-with-edward-cowley

'Buckwheat and Staircase – Auckland Museum', YouTube, 19 February 2020, www.youtube.com/watch?v=tmMbpknUllk

'Carmen's International Coffee Lounge and the Balcony', Museum of New Zealand, www.tepapa.govt.nz/discover-collections/read-watch-play/lgbtqi-histories-aotearoa-new-zealand/carmens-international (accessed 28 February 2024)

Cooper, Justin, 'Polynesian Representation in Drag Inspires Me: Aunty Tamara', Star Observer, 1 August 2023, www.starobserver.com.au/artsentertainment/polynesian-representation-in-drag-inspires-me-aunty-tamara/225343

Hugo Grrrl, 'The Man Behind the King: Hugo Grrrl Documentary', YouTube, 15 July 2019, https://youtu.be/kNNR6yY0z34?si=eVu-w0el9GatujI5

Hansen, Will, 'A Trans History of Gay Liberation in New Zealand', The Spinoff, 27 March 2022, www.thespinoff.co.nz/society/27-03-2022/a-trans-history-of-gay-liberation-in-new-zealand

House of Drag season 1: www.rupaulsdragrace.fandom.com/wiki/House_of_Drag_(Season_1) (accessed 28 February 2024)

House of Drag season 2: www.rupaulsdragrace.fandom.com/wiki/House_of_Drag_(Season_2) (accessed 28 February 2024)
'Kita Mean', www.rupaulsdragrace.fandom.com/wiki/Kita_Mean (accessed 28 February 2024)

Macdonald, Baz, 'The Trials and Triumphs of New Zealand's Drag Kings', RNZ, 6 March 2018, www.rnz.co.nz/news/the-wireless/375157/the-trials-and-triumph-of-new-zealand-s-drag-kings

Richards, Jared, 'Drag Has Become a Little 2D: Drag Race's Refreshing Winner on Refusing to Compromise', Sydney Morning Herald, 21 September 2022, www.smh.com.au/culture/tv-and-radio/drag-has-become-a-little-2d-drag-race-s-refreshing-winner-on-refusing-to-compromise-20220920-p5bjjz.html

Schmidt, Johanna, 'Story: Gender Diversity', Encyclopedia of New Zealand, www.teara.govt.nz/en/gender-diversity (accessed 28 February 2024)

Small, Zane, 'RuPaul's Drag Race Down Under Stars Anita Wigl'it and Yuri Guaii Sit Down to Discuss Going Global', Newshub, 20 October 2022, www.newshub.co.nz/home/entertainment/2022/10/rupaul-s-drag-race-down-under-stars-anita-wigl-it-and-yuri-guaii-sit-down-to-discuss-going-global.html

Townsend, Lynette, 'Story: Rupe, Carmen Tione', Dictionary of New Zealand Biography, 2018, www.teara.govt.nz/en/biographies/6r6/rupe-carmen-tione

Willetts, Cloe, 'House of Drag Winner George Fowler, aka Hugo Grrrl on Being Kiwi Television's First Drag King', Now to Love, 21 December 2018, www.nowtolove.co.nz/lifestyle/career/house-of-drag-george-fowler-hugo-grrrl-drag-king-40102

Williams, Meghan, 'Wellington's "Drag Kings": Comedy, Cabaret and Community', Women's Studies Journal, XXXIV/1–2 (December 2020), pp. 68–75

JAPAN

Danluck, Meredith, and Hayamizu, Yusuke.『ドラァグ・クイーンの素顔 - Drag Queen』. YouTube, VICE Japan, 14 Dec. 2012, https://www.youtube.com/watch?v=k5m6C9WH3b8&t=42s. Accessed 1 Dec. 2022

Delsol, M., & Shinozaki, H. , Edges of the Rainbow: Lgbtq Japan. New Press, 2017.

Fushimi, Noriaki. *Puraibēto Gei Raifu: Posuto Ren'Airon. Gakuyō Shobō*, 1991.
McLelland, Mark J. *Male Homosexuality in Modern Japan: Cultural Myths and Social Realities*. Taylor and Francis, 2005.

McLelland, Mark, et al. Queer Voices from Japan. Lexington Books, 2007.

McLelland, Mark. Queer Japan from the Pacific War to the Internet Age. Rowman & Littlefield, 2005.

McLelland, Mark J., and Wim Lunsing. "The Politics of Okama and Onabe: Uses and Abuses of Terminology Regarding Homosexuality and Transgender." *Genders, Transgenders, and Sexualities in Japan*, Routledge, London, 2006, pp. 81–95

McLelland, Mark, and Katsuhiko Suganuma. "Sexual Minorities and Human Rights in Japan: An Historical Perspective." The International Journal of Human Rights, June 2009. ResearchGate, www.researchgate.net/publication/240521991_Sexual_minorities_and_human_rights_in_Japan_An_historical_perspective.

Senju, K. *Shinjuku Story Vol. 2*. New York, Bard School of the International Center of Photography, 2018.

Suganuma, Katsuhiko. *Contact Moments*. Hong Kong University Press, 2012.

Suganuma, Katsuhiko. "Queering Mainstream Media: Matsuko Deluxe as Modern-Day Kuroko." Routledge Handbook of Japanese Media, ROUTLEDGE, S.l., England, 2020, pp. 169–179

Suganuma, Katsuhiko. "Ways of Speaking About Queer Space in Tokyo: Disorientated Knowledge and Counter Public Space." Japanese Studies, vol. 31, no. 3, 9 Dec. 2011, pp. 345–358., https://doi.org/

Tsukamura, Mami. "【インタビュー】シモーヌ深雪　シャンソン歌手/ドラァグクイーン." *Hanabun Press*, 2020, https://hanabun.press/2020/08/22/simone06/

FRANCE
Berlanstein, Lenard R. "Breeches and Breaches: Cross-Dress Theater and the Culture of Gender Ambiguity in Modern France." *Comparative Studies in Society and History* 38, no. 2 (1996): 338–69. http://www.jstor.org/stable/179132.

Chez Michou. "Son histoire." https://www.michou.com/fr/histoire-du-cabaret/.

Frayssinet, Justine, Marlon Cazanove, Vincent Lamhaut, Charles Delouche Bertolasi, and

Hugo Wintrebert. "Les drag queens font leur grand retour dans les nuits parisiennes." SlateFR. February 10, 2018. https://www.slate.fr/story/157441/nouvelle-vague-drag-queen-paris.
Kondracki, Aziliz & Caillaud, Elias. "En passant à la télé, les drag-queens françaises font bouger les mentalités." *Ouest France*. December 5, 2022. https://www.ouest-france.fr/leditiondusoir/2022-12-05/en-passant-a-la-tele-les-drag-queens-francaises-font-bouger-les-mentalites-af15ef5c-ac1e-4de1-ae07-ca99040347d6.

Millot, Ondine. "The joyous renaissance of Madame Arthur, the very first Parisian drag cabaret." *Le Monde*. July 23, 2022. https://www.lemonde.fr/en/m-le-mag/article/2022/07/23/the-joyous-renaissance-of-madame-arthur-the-very-first-parisian-drag-cabaret_5991211_117.html.

MNC Editorial Team. "Who was the 1920s Moulin Rouge Drag Queen that Inspired Man Ray and Cocteau?" Messy Nessy. February 15, 2023. https://www.messynessychic.com/2023/02/15/who-was-the-1920s-moulin-rouge-drag-queen-that-inspired-man-ray-and-cocteau/.

Philadelphia Museum of Art. "Marcel Duchamp as Rrose Sélavy." https://philamuseum.org/collection/object/56973.

Williamson, Allen. "The Issue of Joan of Arc's Cross-Dressing." *Joan of Arc Archive*. http://archive.joan-of-arc.org/joanofarc_male_clothing.html.

HOLLAND
Galore, L. *interview*, January 2, 2024. https://drive.google.com/drive/u/0/folders/1NRfD-OUtRtI5gpOSW5Inj3SLcj6ruoiM

Grijp, L. P. (2006). Boys and female impersonators in the Amsterdam theatre of the seventeenth century. *Medieval English Theatre*, 28, pp131–170. Boys and female impersonators in the Amsterdam theatre of the seventeenth century.

Hekma, G., & Duyvendak, J. W. (2011). Queer Netherlands: A puzzling example. Sexualities, 14(6), 625-631. https://doi.org/10.1177/1363460711422303

Hekma, G. (2013). Amsterdam⊠s Sexual Underground in the 1960s. In C. Lindner & A. Hussey (Eds.), *Paris-Amsterdam Underground: Essays on Cultural Resistance, Subversion, and Diversion* (pp. 49–62). Amsterdam University Press. http://www.jstor.org/stable/j.ctt6wp6td.8

Hofman, Paul, 'Victoria False: Ik Breek Lans voor Roze Ouderen', Pride Amsterdam (accessed February 2024)

Hopelezz, Jennifer, (n.d.). *Jennifer Hopelezz*.

https://www.houseofhopelezz.com/

Jacobs, L. (2017). Regulating the Reguliers: How the Normalization of Gays and Lesbians in Dutch Society Impacts LGBTQ Nightlife. *Independent Study Project (ISP) Collection*. 2651. https://digitalcollections.sit.edu/isp_collection/2651

Johansen, P.R. personal communication, January 10, 2024.

I Amsterdam. (2023, July 19). *Amsterdam's sparkling drag scene*. I amsterdam. https://www.iamsterdam.com/en/whats-on/theatre-and-stage/amsterdams-sparkling-drag-scene

Korcek, M. (2010). Drag Kinging in Amsterdam: Queer Identity Politics, Subcultural Spaces, and Transformative Potentials. *Lawrence University Honors Projects*. 116. https://lux.lawrence.edu/luhp/116

Kuiper, L. M., de Ruijter, A., & van Waesberghe, B. S. (2016, January 26). Bert's logbook: Informal care during the 80s and 90s AIDS epidemic in Amsterdam. Public History Amsterdam. https://publichistory.humanities.uva.nl/queercollection/berts-logbook-informal-care-during-the-80s-and-90s-aids-epidemic-in-amsterdam/

About Us (2023, November 3). Dragshow Bar Lellebel. https://www.lellebel.nl/about-us/

Wiki, C. T. R. D. R. (n.d.). *Make Up Your Mind*. RuPaul's Drag Race Wiki. https://rupaulsdragrace.fandom.com/wiki/Make_Up_Your_Mind

Wiki, C. T. R. D. R. (n.d.). *Envy Peru*. RuPaul's Drag Race Wiki. https://rupaulsdragrace.fandom.com/wiki/Envy_Peru

Milkshake Festival | 29 & 30 July 2023 Westerpark Amsterdam. (n.d.). *Milkshake Festival*. https://www.milkshakefestival.com/about

Victoria False - *Pride Amsterdam*. (2020, March 30). Pride Amsterdam. https://pride.amsterdam/ambassadors/victoria-false/

SWEDEN
We'd like to acknowledge Sam Message of Status Queer who provided some very helpful insights for this chapter.

UNITED KINGDOM
Abou Nasr, Gaelle, 'The Evolution of Drag: A History of Self-expressionism', *By Arcadia*, 12 December 2021, www.byarcadia.org/post/the-evolution-of-drag-a-history-of-self-expressionism

Hall, Jake, 'The Surprising Story of Princess Seraphina, England's Earliest Drag Queen',

Them, 24 August 2023, www.them.us/story/princess-seraphina-englands-earliest-drag-queen-essay

Harper, Douglas, 'Drag', *Online Etymology Dictionary*, www.etymonline.com/word/drag#etymonline_v_15871 (accessed 5 November 2023)

'List of *Little Britain* Characters', Wikipedia, https://en.wikipedia.org/w/index.php?title=List_of_Little_Britain_characters (accessed 6 November 2023)

Quinn, James 'La Rue, Danny', *Dictionary of Irish Biography* (June 2015; revised February 2019), www.dib.ie/biography/la-rue-danny-a9721

Thorpe, Vanessa, 'Secret Lives of Women Who Broke Taboo Act in Shakespeare', *The Guardian*, 10 April 2016, www.theguardian.com/culture/2016/apr/10/secret-lives-of-women-shakespeare

Tonic, Gina, 'Meet the Drag Artist Inspo behind *Everybody's Talking about Jamie*', *i-D*, 6 November 2020

Victoria and Albert Museum, 'The Story of Pantomime', www.vam.ac.uk/articles/the-story-of-pantomime (accessed 6 November 2023)

CANADA

A Gay Ole Time – A Celebration of Newfoundland's Gay History. (2022, August 4). 43 years ago this week in the summer of 1979 2 drag queens invaded the shores of Quidi Vidi Lake and set up a Kissing booth [Video]. Facebook. https://www.facebook.com/watch/?v=618643872902728

Allaire, C. (2020, August 31). *Indigenous Queen Ilona Verley On Bringing Two-Spirit Representation to Canada's Drag Race*. VOGUE. Retrieved March 31, 2023, from https://www.vogue.com/article/ilona-verley-canadas-drag-race-indigenous-queen

Allen, K. (2014, January 23). *Club Carousel – Our Community's Foundation*. Calgary Gay History Project. Retrieved May 22, 2023, from https://calgarygayhistory.ca/2014/01/23/club-carousel-our-communitys-foundation/

Bonnell, Y. (2023) @Yolanda_Bonnell. July 15. Available at: https://twitter.com/Yolanda_Bonnell/status/1680340656911204353 (Accessed July 16, 2023).

Burnett, R. (2022, July 29). The Evolution of Drag in Montreal, and How RuPaul Changed the Game. Montreal Gazette. Retrieved April 29, 2023, from https://montrealgazette.com/entertainment/local-arts/the-evolution-of-drag-in-montreal-and-how-rupaul-changed-the-game

Britannica (1998, July 20). *Julian Eltinge: American Vaudeville Star*. Britannica Arts & Culture. Retrieved June 18, 2023, from https://www.britannica.com/biography/Julian-Eltinge

Canadian Expeditionary Force Research Group (2020, October 3). The Dumbells *Concert Party in the Great War*. CEFRG. Retrieved July 4, 2023, from https://cefrg.ca/blog/the-dumbells-concert-party/

Canadian Broadcasting Corporation (2021, June 13). *Winnipeg Cree influencer featured in Sephora's first Indigenous history month ad campaign*. CBC. Retrieved March 12, 2023, from https://www.cbc.ca/news/canada/manitoba/sephora-canada-indigenous-campaign-winnipeg-1.6064227

Canadian Broadcasting Corporation (2016, November 24). *Meet Michelle DuBarry, Canada's oldest performing drag queen*. CBC. Retrieved March 19, 2023, from https://www.cbc.ca/radio/noworsever/how-to-rock-your-golden-years-1.3862134/meet-michelle-dubarry-canada-s-oldest-performing-drag-queen-1.3862361

Clapson, D. (2022, February 26). *Drag performers are building an audience on the Prairies*. The Globe and Mail. Retrieved March 11, 2023.

Curtis, H. (2021, June 17). Urban Oral History: Understanding The Village of 1970s and 80s, Part III. *Spacing*. http://spacing.ca/toronto/2021/06/17/urban-oral-history-understanding-the-village-of-1970s-and-80s-part-iii/

East, P. (2003, August 20). *Rusty Ryan*. Xtra. Retrieved June 2, 2023, from https://xtramagazine.com/culture/rusty-ryan-43407

Flare (n.d.). *1995 – Present • Flare*. Drag King History. Retrieved July 3, 2023, from https://dragkinghistory.com/1995-present-flare/

Government of Canada (2022, November 3). *History of RCMP-2SLGBTQI+ relations*. Royal Canadian Mounted Police. Retrieved May 14, 2023, from https://www.rcmp-grc.gc.ca/en/history-rcmp-2slgbtqi-relations

Hagen, D. (2007). *The Edmonton Queen: The Final Voyage* (1st ed., pp. 78-79). Brindle & Glass.

Hagen, D. (2021, May 18). *After the Pisces Bathhouse Raid: Millie – I'm Number One*. City Museum Edmonton. Retrieved July 17, 2023, from https://citymuseumedmonton.ca/2021/05/18/after-the-pisces-bathhouse-raid-millie-im-number-one/

Hays, M. (2019, November 18). *Raiding History*. The Walrus. Retrieved June 10, 2023, from https://thewalrus.ca/raiding-history/

Latimer, K. (2022, June 23). *First Nations Drag Artist is 1st Queen from Sask. Competing to be Canada's Next Drag Superstar*. CBC News.

Retrieved March 12, 2023, from https://www.cbc.ca/news/canada/saskatchewan/sask-drag-queen-canada-drag-race-1.6497705

Levy, R. (2020, August 21). *We Demand*. The Canadian Encyclopedia. Retrieved May 6, 2023, from https://www.thecanadianencyclopedia.ca/en/article/we-demand

Lewis, L. (2017, July 20). *Happy Ours: A History of Local Gay Bars*. The Coast. Retrieved April 11, 2023, from https://www.thecoast.ca/arts-music/happy-ours-a-history-of-local-gay-bars-8492071#:~:text=The%20first%20%E2%80%9Cofficially%20gay%E2%80%9D%20gay,in%20this%20story%20was%20sourced

Mackie, J. (2017, November 24). This Week in History: 1927 A 'Modified Spanish Renaissance' theatre opens on Granville Street. *Vancouver Sun*. https://vancouversun.com/news/local-news/this-week-in-history-1927-a-modified-spanish-renaissance-theatre-opens-on-granville-street

Martin, R. (2021, June 17). *Your Guide To Drag Scenes Across Canada (Beyond Toronto, Montreal & Vancouver)*. FASHION. Retrieved March 28, 2023, from https://fashionmagazine.com/style/drag-scenes-canada/

Mutabdzija Jaksic, V. (2020, August 26). *The History of Drag on Screen: Strutting From Ancient Times to CBC's Queens*. CBC. Retrieved May 26, 2023.

Phair, M. (2014, September 16). *Flashback and the Gay Drag Races*. City Museum Edmonton. Retrieved March 10, 2023, from https://citymuseumedmonton.ca/2014/09/16/flashback-and-the-gay-drag-races/

Pratt, W. J. (2012, October 19). *War is a Drag: Female Impersonators in the First World War*. O Canadian History. Retrieved April 14, 2023, from http://ocanadianhistory.blogspot.com/2012/10/war-is-drag-female-impersonators-in.html

Rotinga, R. (2023, June 24). *A Century Ago, This Star 'Female Impersonator' Made Men Swoon*. Washington Post. Retrieved July 6, 2023, from https://www.washingtonpost.com/history/2023/06/25/drag-queen-julian-eltinge-broadway/

Salerno, R. (2011, August 7). *'I like when you can tame the fear out of people'*. Xtra. Retrieved March 18, 2023, from https://xtramagazine.com/culture/i-like-when-you-can-tame-the-fear-out-of-people-33713

Sherry, P. (2020, October 26). *A City Untucked: Drag History in Montreal*. The Link. Retrieved May 13, 2023, from https://thelinknewspaper.ca/article/a-city-untucked-drag-history-in-montreal

Sky, P., Talia, F., Stallion, A., Lo, B., & Honey, L. (2020, December 3). *The Birth of The Bannock Babes and a Drag Community*. Canadian Art. Retrieved March 23, 2023, from https://canadianart.ca/interviews/the-birth-of-the-bannock-babes-and-a-drag-community/

Smyth, C. (n.d.). *1978-Present Crema*. Drag King History. Retrieved March 19, 2023, from https://dragkinghistory.com/1978-present-crema/

Stevenson, V. (2015, November 29). *Toronto's Oldest Drag Queen Takes World Record*. The Toronto Star. Retrieved March 29, 2023, from https://www.thestar.com/news/gta/toronto-s-oldest-drag-queen-takes-world-record/article_5732d3d8-f3b7-509f-bdd7-0720e3b1089c.html

The University of Guelph (2012, November 8). *Actor Soldiers Lifted Morale in First World War*. University of Guelph News. Retrieved April 24, 2023, from https://news.uoguelph.ca/2012/11/actor-soldiers-lifted-morale-in-first-world-war/

The University of Manitoba (2020, January 30). *Meeting Places*. Manitoba Gay and Lesbian Archives. Retrieved May 15, 2023, from https://libguides.lib.umanitoba.ca/c.php?g=703093&p=4998172#:~:text=In%20late%201970%2C%20the%20first,club%20with%20no%20liquor%20license

Tkach, G. (n.d.). *The Orpheum and Its Drag Queens*. Forbidden Vancouver. Publishing date unknown. Retrieved June 14, 2023, from https://forbiddenvancouver.ca/blog/the-orpheum-and-its-drag-queens/

Tkach, G. (2019, July 6). *Vancouver's Hidden History: A Drag Queen's Fight for Decriminalization*. The Daily Hive. Retrieved May 29, 2023, from https://dailyhive.com/vancouver/vancouver-history-ted-northe

(n.d.). *Toronto's Drag History*. Feel Your Fantasy. Retrieved July 2, 2023, from https://feelyourfantasy.com/pages/toronto-drag-history

Viegas, M. (2019, June 26). *One of the World's Oldest Drag Queens Shares Memories of Life in Toronto in the 1950s*. FASHION. Retrieved May 6, 2023, from https://fashionmagazine.com/flare/celebrity/michelle-dubarry-oldest-drag-queen-canada/

"VIDEO: 'We Demand'," *The Village Legacy Project | Le Projet de legs du village*, accessed July 18, 2023, https://www.villagelegacy.ca/items/show/8.

(n.d.). Wonderful Grand Band. Citizen Freak. Retrieved March 31, 2023, from https://citizenfreak.com/artists/105428-wonderful-grand-band

https://www.cbc.ca/comedy/the-history-of-drag-on-screen-strutting-from-ancient-times-to-cbc-s-queens-1.5699542

https://www.theglobeandmail.com/canada/alberta/article-drag-performers-are-building-an-audience-in-the-at-prairie-venues/

BRAZIL

https://amauryjr.blog.bol.uol.com.br/2022/07/04/drag-brunch-brasil-chega-a-sao-paulo-com-apresentacao-de-ikaro-kadoshi/

https://buzzfeed.com.br/post/16-coisas-que-voce-provavelmente-nao-sabia-sobre-a-elke-maravilha

https://www.cartacapital.com.br/diversidade/bate-cabelo-vai-alem-da-danca-e-vira-ato-de-forca-para-lgbts-assista/

https://culturaemcasa.com.br/video/sao-paulo-em-hi-fi/

https://draglicious.com.br/2020/06/03/conheca-miss-bia-pioneira-drag-queen-brasileira/

https://www.estadao.com.br/emais/gente/epa-bicha-nao-15-anos-sem-jorge-lafond-a-vera-verao/

https://gauchazh.clicrbs.com.br/cultura-e-lazer/almanaque/noticia/2021/01/conheca-a-historia-da-flower-s-a-primeira-boate-gay-da-capital-ckjyknc0r005a019wta5hdn8e.html

https://gauchazh.clicrbs.com.br/donna/noticia/2015/09/com-a-cara-no-sol-fenomeno-das-drag-queens-conquista-espaco-cativo-na-noite-de-porto-alegre-cjplg7i9t01c4mncn2376gvwz.html

https://g1.globo.com/sp/sao-paulo/noticia/2020/06/03/miss-bia-drag-queen-pioneira-no-brasil-morre-vitima-de-covid-19-em-sp-aos-80-anos.ghtml

https://www1.folha.uol.com.br/saopaulo/2014/02/1408677-nostromondo-primeira-boate-gay-do-brasil-fecha-as-portas-apos-43-anos.shtml

https://www.jornaldocomercio.com/_conteudo/especiais/reportagem_cultural/2022/05/848521-a-historia-da-flowers-primeira-boate-gay-de-porto-alegre.html

https://medium.com/@dnareporter/nilton-j%C3%BAnior-a-cassandra-calabou%C3%A7o-3c54cff9d02d

https://memoriascinematograficas.com.br/2021/01/relembrando-o-talentoso-e-irreverente-jorge-lafond-epaaa.html

https://www.otvfoco.com.br/fez-historia-o-talkshow-que-elke-maravilha-teve-em-1993-no-sbt-e-tratou-de-assuntos-como-homofobia-e-racismo/

https://primeirosnegros.com/madame-sata-uma-travesti-artista-militante/

https://revistaladoa.com.br/2009/03/gente/ode-uma-estrela-rebecca-mcdonald/

https://www.revistalofficiel.com.br/pop-culture/ikaro-kadoshi-em-entrevista-exclusiva-para-l-officiel-confira

https://revistaquem.globo.com/capas/noticia/2023/06/marcia-pantera-a-precursora-do-bate-cabelo-cai-levantei-mas-nao-deixei-de-sonhar.ghtml

https://revistaquem.globo.com/capas/noticia/2023/06/silvetty-montilla-o-humor-me-ajuda-fico-feliz-em-ver-as-pessoas-rindo-com-o-que-faco.ghtml

https://www.silvanatoazza.com.br/noticias/detalhe/charlene-voluntaire-e-voluntaria-da-volupia

https://storymaps.arcgis.com/stories/be0af8c464774ec38d9dda14d85b33f4

https://www.terra.com.br/nos/paradasp/conheca-ikaro-kadoshi-um-dos-maiores-nomes-do-cenario-drag-queen-do-brasil,52d75d519294c30915b7b21aff67af67famr3hlz.html

https://www.ufrgs.br/grafiadrag/gloria-crystal/

https://universoretro.com.br/a-vida-de-madame-sata-o-bicha-mais-macho-do-brasil/

https://pt.wikipedia.org/wiki/Condessa_M%C3%B4nica

https://pt.wikipedia.org/wiki/Dzi_Croquettes

https://www.youtube.com/watch?v=IBVa4VnDMc0

SUPPORTING LOCAL DRAG

You'll find on these pages small nuggets of advice for visiting each of the countries featured in this book, from the hottest spots to if and how you should tip.

AUSTRALIA
The Sydney Gay and Lesbian Mardi Gras is an annual celebration for the LGBTQ+ community in Australia. Celebrations and events typically start at the beginning of February and continue right through the month culminating in the world-famous Mardi Gras parade on the first Saturday in March.

NEW ZEALAND
New Zealand's smaller population in itself forms part of the drag community's charm. Small budgets mean that often, as well as seeing drag artists perform, you may also see them selling tickets at the door, playing the music and packing away at the end!

JAPAN
Key venues in Tokyo are found mainly in Shinjuku Ni-chōme: Aiiro (an open-air bar where queens dance in the street), Alamas, Aisotope, Campy! and Eagle Tokyo Blue. Outside of Ni-chōme, drag performers populate high production events such as Department H, Casket of Horrors, Fresh Meat and Opulence. Osaka drag bars include Do With Cafe, Lip Service, Ludo and Explosion, while Nagoya's queens host, bartend and perform at Bar Piece, Queen Diamond, Kimagurecats and The Metro Club (at LOVER:z). Last but not least, when in Kyoto do not miss the celebrated *Diamonds Are Forever* show.

Tipping is greatly appreciated! Some queens carry buckets so patrons can 'make it hail' with 100 and 500 yen coins (equivalent to $1 and $5).

THE PHILIPPINES
A staple of the drag scene in the Philippines, don't miss seeing The Golden Gays perform, a community of older gay men and drag elders who live together in a house in Pasay City. They are affectionately called *lolas* (grandmothers in Filipino).

THAILAND
As the birthplace of drag in Thailand, Pattaya has many cabaret style shows, where queens compete to win crowns and money, including the standout Tiffany's Show. These are typically more family-friendly and are accessible for both queer and straight audiences.

FRANCE
If you wish to dip your toe into the past, the iconic facade of Madame Arthur has been maintained and its cabaret style performances, music shows, drag performances and dance nights continue to make the surrounding area of Paris a vibrant queer hotspot, harking back to some of the country's earliest drag and queer performers.

GERMANY
If you're in Munich, one of the two key centres of drag in Germany, along with Berlin, why not try its monthly lip-sync competition, *Lovers Lipsync*, hosted by Pinay Colada and one of the first competitions open to all types of artists.

ITALY
To experience Milan's infamous alternative scene, embark on a trip to Toilet Club, an inclusive, no dress code underground party, with a drag show that features drag queens, kings, creatures and burlesque performers. There are no rules on genre or performance type, and there is an open stage to kick off the night, and two rooms with different genres of music. In Rome, the biggest drag night is Muccassassina, which started in 1991 and is now the country's longest-running LGBTQ+ party.

HOLLAND
Keep an eye out for The Drag Olympics and Superball, the two climactic events of the Dutch drag calendar year. The Milkshake Festival is a highlight performance event, and there are many options for diverse drag tastes, from the traditional drag of Queen's Head to the edgier drag of Club Church.

SPAIN
Spanish clubs and venues often announce their drag shows a week or two in advance, and there are drag parties every weekend in Barcelona or Madrid. Iconiqa is a huge one, visited very often by international queens. However, the best way to catch shows is simply by following your favourites on social media, and falling into their drag rabbit hole. A cultural note: tipping is not customary, and some shows can start past midnight!

SWEDEN
There is only one rule about what drag performers can do onstage, and that is that they can do anything they want! Lip-syncs, dance, stand-up, theatre, monologues, singing, impersonations and even more can be seen on stages across the country.

UNITED KINGDOM
In the UK, the main hotspots for LGBTQIA+ nightlife are Cardiff, Edinburgh, London, Brighton and Manchester.

Tipping culture does not exist in the UK. It is limited even in bars and restaurants as the smallest bill is £5, and tipping coins is impractical for both the performer and the attendees.

CANADA
Canadian show etiquette is unique. Tipping is customary, but the smallest bill is $5. There are $1 and $2 coins – loonies and toonies – but these require a tip bucket; a handful of change is impolite. Quebec is the outlier, as until recently Quebecois queens didn't want cash tips. Those were traditionally for strip clubs and were considered an insult to drag entertainers who didn't want to be conflated due to outdated stigmatization of sex work. However, more people tip here as drag popularizes.

UNITED STATES
In New York, venues range from small, casual spots like The Rosemont or Metropolitan, to huge venues with the capacity to host grand theatrical events, like 3 Dollar Bill or House of Yes.

The United States is a tipping economy. Since Covid and the popularization of banking apps like Venmo or CashApp, performers may be able to accept digital tips, but as many Americans do not have access to banks, cash is your best option for making sure performers head home with compensation for their work.

BRAZIL
Popular nightclubs include Blue Space, Eagle São Paulo and Tunnel in São Paulo, and Vitraux Indiscretus and Work Room Bar in Porto Alegre.

Brazil does not have a 'tipping culture', as it is not part of the wider culture in the country. Everything is included in the original price!

ABOUT THE AUTHORS

Zephyr Aspen (he/they) is a trans man who does drag under the name of Rose Quartz (they/them) in the UK and in NYC. He was published many times between the ages of 13 and 18 through Young Writers and is currently querying his first full-length adult novel.
You can find him on social media: @rosequartzdrag

Sara Altea Balestra has been immersed in LGBTQ+ activism from a young age, with experience of the drag scenes in many different countries, mainly Italy and the United States, where she has lived. She holds a degree in animal welfare and a diploma in translation for cinema and television. The two combine in her work as a translator, for companies committed to environmental protection. She also occasionally writes theatre reviews and works as an event photographer.

Courtney Conquers is a Canadian drag performer and writer who specializes in drag media archiving and live events. She is best known as a co-creator of the queer media collective Drag Coven. Courtney has a Master of Arts in Women's and Gender Studies and is an outspoken advocate for equity in drag and queer spaces. Her time as part of Drag Coven has enabled her to witness and film drag across the world, working with countless people among drag's biggest names along the way. Drag Coven, the first of its kind, is currently the world's biggest contemporary, free online drag media archive.
You can find her on social media: @courtneyconquer
Drag Coven: @dragcoven

Javier Izquierdo Cubas has been working as a translator for various events in Spain that showcase international guests since 2021. Within this environment predominantly composed of local drag queens and members of the queer community, Javier has successfully distinguished and adapted the perks and nuances of the Spanish drag glossary to the English language.
Javier would like to thank: Rosario Molina, Xess, La Caneli, Nacha Bohéme, Prisma Lux, Kimera, Mary Conazo, Marcus Massalami, Álvaro Panda

Kat Joplin is a journalist and fiction writer from San Diego, USA, now based in Tokyo. They perform internationally as the queen 'Le Horla', and are a member of ballroom House of Mizrahi and the drag Haus von Schwarz. Kat graduated Stanford University in 2015 with a bachelor's in creative writing and Japanese, and from Waseda University with a master's studying Japan's drag queen culture. They now cover much of Japan's English language drag media for publications such as *Gay Times*, *Japan Times*, *Tokyo Weekender*, and *Them* magazine.
Social Media: @kat_dearu

Tsarlotte Lucifer is a Munich-based, Manila-born, and New York-raised drag rockstar and a new writer. She grew up surrounded by the arts and literature, and started drag in 2018 after moving to Germany with her family. Her background as a Filipino trans woman doing drag in Europe informs a lot of her work, and she's done it all; from comedy, to music, to poetry, and everything in between. You can find her around Germany rocking on stages and smoking in the back.

Alex Nolos is a trans writer, editor and drag king born and residing in Brooklyn. He is the author of Cut and Save the Line, a novel, and his work has been published in Catapult, Hominum Journal and Wrongdoing Magazine. In 2013, he was awarded 'Best-Looking Cross-Dresser' by his classmates.
Social media: @alexnolos on Instagram, @riporsonprice (drag) on Twitter and Instagram
Website: alexnolos.com

Courtney Norton is a pop culture enthusiast and writer from Brisbane, Australia. She has a Bachelor of Journalism and a Bachelor of Arts from the University of Queensland. Throughout her career she has written for a number of publications across a variety of industries including Queensland Brides, Holidays for Couples, Frooty and Scenestr. When she's not brainstorming about who and what will be the next big thing in pop culture, Courtney enjoys exploring the world; taking in as much drag performance from as many different places as she can.

Gigi Rajkumar Guerandi is a young South African writer and journalist, residing between Copenhagen, New York City and Cape Town. They hold three degrees across various fields, including a master's degree in journalism from Columbia University. They primarily work within narrative non-fiction, long-form feature writing and short-form documentary filmmaking. Their encyclopedic knowledge of queer culture in twentieth century media has led them to believe they are the queerest person alive. You can find Gigi on social media @_giuseppeguerandi.

Jeffrey Rowe currently lives in Montreal, Canada. He completed his master's degree in history at McGill University where he studied Canadian Spiritualism in the nineteenth and early twentieth centuries. When he's not at his desk writing or playing video games, Jeffrey spends his time with family and friends or quietly lounging with a novel in hand.

Juliana Santos, or Juli, as she prefers to be called, also goes by her drag name Nasty Queen. Her main job is dog walker/pet sitter but she also has a bachelor's degree in public relations and went on to receive a master's in criminal profiling.

Viktor 'Caffeine' Skancke, a Swedish-Norwegian copywriter and content producer, grew up tasting all kinds of culture. Hit by the magic of drag 2004, along with most of their generation, their love for the art grew together with their passion for storytelling, something they claim drag is an excellent platform for. Fascinated by human interaction and using culture as a mean of communication they are a scholar of enjoying, observing and supporting drag, queer culture and embracing the past to move toward the future.

Presley Stewart (she/they) is a writer, student of film and television at Columbia College, Chicago, and, of course, a fierce lover of all things queer and drag-related since the day she was born. They are so excited to shine a light on the colourful and vibrant community that is Thailand's drag scene.

INDEX

Page numbers in *italics* refer to images

PICTURE CREDITS

2 Photo Drag Coven (2021) **7** Photo Sean Vadella **8** Photo Quinton Cruickshanks (2019) **10** Eric Weiss/WWD/Penske Media/Getty Images **13** Photo Drag Coven **16** Photo Greg Bailey @gregbaileyphoto **19** Peter Parks/AFP/Getty Images **20** Photo Mark Dickson, Deep Field Photography **22** PictureLux/The Hollywood Archive/Alamy Stock Photo **23** Fairfax Media/Getty Images **24** Kevin John Berry/Sydney Morning Herald/Getty Images **26** Tara Ziemba/Getty Images **27** Photo courtesy Team Timber Productions **28** Self Portrait. Image courtesy Kita Mean **31** © The copyright holder, Te Papa (O.044281) **32** The Dominion Post Collection, Alexander Turnbull Library, Wellington, New Zealand (23041778) **33** Photo TNS Studio. Image courtesy Spankie Jackzon **34** Photo Lane Worral. Image courtesy Hugo Grrrl **35** Historic Collection/Alamy Stock Photo **36** © The copyright holder, Te Papa (GH011913) **37** Steven Saphore/Australia Associated Press/Alamy Stock Photo **39** Fiona Goodall/Getty Images **40** Photo UTO **42** Jack Vartoogian/Getty Images **43** Associated Press/Alamy Stock Photo **44** Art Theatre Guild/Matsumoto Production Company/Album/Alamy Stock Photo **46** Image courtesy Club METRO, Kyoto **47** Yoshio Tsunoda/Aflo Co. Ltd./Alamy Stock Photo **48** Michael Judd (Belgium Solanas) and Shannon Lester (Sasha Zamolodchikova) **49** Photo Alejandro Morales Rama **51** Photo Akane Kiyohara **52** Image courtesy Taylor Sheesh **54** Chronicle/Alamy Stock Photo **55** Jay Directo/AFP/Getty Images **56** MARKOVA Comfort Gay, 2000 directed by Gil M. Portes, RVQ Productions, restored by Central Digital Lab Inc. Poster artwork by Justin Besana **57** Sarah Morris/WireImage/Getty Images **58–59** Chelsea Guglielmino/Getty Images **60** Noel Celis/AFP/Getty Images **61** Photo Elroe Banawa at Jagger Studio. Image courtesy Myx Chanel **62** Photo Meghan Tuy and Vien Syjongtian Image courtesy Inah Demons **64** Santiago Felipe/Getty Images **66** Panther Media GmbH/Alamy Stock Photo **67** John Warburton-Lee Photography/Alamy Stock Photo **68** Pito A. Sahakorn/LightRocket/Getty Images **69** Cinematic/Alamy Stock Photo **70** Image Professionals GmbH/Alamy Stock Photo **72–73** Jewel Samad/AFP/Getty Images **74** asiandelight/Shutterstock **75** GUIDENOP/Shutterstock **76** Photo Dylan Perlot. Image courtesy Nicky Doll **79** DeAgostini/Getty Images **80** Robert Lasquin, 'Mme. Arthur' Program, 1950. Digital Transgender Archive (mg74qm30x) **81** The Metropolitan Museum of Art, New York, Harris Brisbane Dick Fund, 1932 (32.88.12) **82** David Wharry/BIPs/Getty Images **83** Gaston Paris/Roger Viollet/Getty Images **84** Pierre Verdy/Getty Images **87** Astrid Stawiarz/Getty Images **88** Photo Merlyn Charles Nieto. Image courtesy Barbie Q **90** Prismatic Pictures/Bridgeman Images **91** carnivalpix/Alamy Stock Photo **92** Image courtesy Jazz Cortes **94** Photo Anne Coersmeier. Image courtesy Daphny Ryan, Matthias Niederlechner **95** Photo Merlyn Charles Nieto. Image courtesy Medi Ocre **96** Photo Ilayda Dağlı. Image courtesy LéLé Cocoon **98** Photo Ilayda Dağlı. Image courtesy LéLé Cocoon. **98** Hannes Magerstaedt/Getty Images **99** Drag Star NRW. Düsseldorfer Schauspielhaus. Photo Melanie Zanin **100** Image courtesy La Diamond and Goudie Events **103** Rino Petrosino/Mondadori/Getty Images **105** Fototeca Gilardi/Getty Images **106, 107** Image courtesy Centro di Documentazione Marco Sanna del Circolo Mario Mieli **108–109** Photo Paolo Lombardo. Image courtesy Karma B: Carmelo Pappalardo and Mauro Leonardi **110** Mondadori/Getty Images **112** Photo Jelle Pieter de Boer. Image courtesy Lady Galore **115** Photo Joost Evers/Anefo/National Archives, The Hague (2.24.01.03) **116** Joy Publications **117** Jerry Lampen/AFP/Getty Images **118** Photo Cyriel Jacobs. Image courtesy Envy Peru **120** Photo Jelle Pieter de Boer. Image courtesy Lady Galore **121** Eva Plevier/Alamy Stock Photo **122** Photo Michel Swart Photography. Image courtesy Jennifer Hopelezz **123** Photo Rémon van den Kommer. Image courtesy Jennifer Hopelezz **124** Photo Álvaro Panda **126** Darling Archive/Alamy Stock Photo **128** David Benito/Getty Images **129** Prodicciones Zeta/Album/Alamy Stock Photo **130** Image courtesy Drag Sethlas **133** Aldara Zarraoa/Redferns/Getty Images **134** Photo Pedro Bejar; Creative Director Isabeau Garabito. Image courtesy The Macarena **135** Photo Satnof - @satnof_ **136** Photo David Gabrielron. Image courtesy Elecktra **138** *Long Live Little Märta* by Hasse Ekman, 1945, Terrafilms Productions. Image courtesy The Swedish Film Database, Swedish Film Institute **139** Blekinge Museum, Kariskrona (Blm_JLind 058) **140** Photo Peter Kjellerås/Aftonbladet **141** Image courtesy Babsan **142–143** Photo Andreas Nilsson. Image courtesy Sofia Södergård/Qarl Qunt **144** Photo Peter Knutson **146** Image courtesy Status Queer **147** Image courtesy Annie Lööf and Anton Engström **148** Dan Burn-Forti/Contour/Getty Images **150** Chronicle/Alamy Stock Photo **151** Nobby Clark/Popperfoto/Getty Images **152** Vibrant Pictures/Alamy Stock Photo **153** Yale Center for British Art, Paul Mellon Collection (B1977.14.11245) **154** United News/Popperfoto/Getty Images **155** Odile Noel/Alamy Stock Photo **156–157** Image courtesy Pecs Drag Kings **158** Mickey Rooney/Alamy Stock Photo **159** Anthony Devlin/Getty Images **160** *Canada's Drag Race* season 4 winner VENUS photographed by The Drag Series / @TheDragSeries **162** Canada Department of National Defence/Library and Archives Canada (1964-114-NPC) **163** *National Vaudeville Artists Souvenir*, 1923 New York. Media History Digital Library, Wisconsin Center for Film & Theater Research **164** Image courtesy QMUNITY **166** Photo Drag Coven (2024) **169** Chelsea Guglielmino/Getty Images **170** Melissa Renwick/Toronto Star/Getty Images **171** Photo Drag Coven (2021) **172** Photo D.J. Lehrhaupt **174** Stephanie Keith/Getty Images **175** Photo Mettie Ostrowski. Image courtesy Switch n' Play **176** La Zavaleta presents Bitchfest at CmonEverybody. Photo Anthony Leo Photography **178** Emory Libraries, Emory University, Atlanta (MSS1218_B074_I253) **179** Rose Leechs **180** Sarah Morris/WireImage/Getty Images **182** Richard Vogel/Associated Press/Alamy Stock Photo **184** Photo Rodolfo Corradin. Image courtesy Lorelay Fox **187** Arquivo Nacional Collection, Rio De Janeiro, Public Domain **188** Image courtesy Franco Araujo **189** Yuri Murakami/Foto Area LRDA/Alamy Stock Photo **190** Diogo Baptista/Alamy Stock Photo **191** Buda Mendes/LatinContent/Getty Images **192** Berenice Bautista/Associated Press/Alamy Stock Photo **195** Photo Pedro Karg @pedrokarg_fotografo

On the Jacket: **FRONT** Gottmik, Photo Albert Sanchez and Pedro Zalba / **BACK** Photo Paolo Lombardo. Image courtesy Karma B: Carmelo Pappalardo and Mauro Leonardi

ACKNOWLEDGEMENTS

For my part, *Planet Drag* was written amidst chaos. Over the course of its evolution, my pieces were brought to life quite literally on planes, trains and automobiles; during tours, between gigs and in stolen moments at my day jobs. My research and writing took place during every hour of the day and night while I tried to keep all the plates in the air and spinning. I felt a genuine connection with the time-honoured drag tradition of doing what you've gotta do – whenever and wherever you've gotta do it – to make things happen.

Planet Drag wouldn't have been possible without the queens who raised me – and I mean that in several contexts:

My moms – my actual mom and my drag mom Chiffon – for fielding my stress texts.

The group chat – Jamie, Juice, and Perla – who ... also fielded my stress texts.

Brooke Lynn who ... well ... also fielded my stress texts!

All the other queens, kings and things who listened to me geek out about this project, told me they were proud of me or have otherwise influenced my journey in drag; I'm so lucky to know the amazing artists I do.

Thank you to the team at Quarto for approaching me, encouraging me and being patient with the ever-changing tornado that is my schedule. Thank you to my contributors, who were an absolute delight to work with; I'm thrilled to have learned from each and every one of you. Thank you to the queens, artists and scholars who helped my writers with their own chapters; our book would be nothing without your knowledge, guidance and experience.

Finally, thank you to my beautiful girlfriend Lexi, for fielding my stress texts, but mostly for reading all of my versions, hyping me up daily, keeping me laughing and being my peace. I love you the most.

Quarto

First published in 2024 by White Lion Publishing,
an imprint of The Quarto Group.
One Triptych Place
London, SE1 9SH,
United Kingdom
T (0)20 7700 6700
www.Quarto.com

A catalogue record for this book is available from the British Library.

ISBN 978-0-7112-9072-3
Ebook ISBN 978-0-7112-9073-0

10 9 8 7 6 5 4 3 2 1

Design by Leonardo Collina

Cover photo of Gottmik by Albert Sanchez and Pedro Zalba

Publisher: Jessica Axe
Commissioning Editor: Andrew Roff
Editor: Katerina Menhennet
Production Controller: Rohana Yusof

Printed in China